D1544899

Understanding

The Crucible

New and future titles in the Understanding Great Literature series include:

Understanding

The Crucible

UNDERSTANDING GREAT LITERATURE

M.N. Jimerson

LUCENT
BOOKS®

THOMSON
————★————™
GALE

San Diego • Detroit • New York • San Francisco • Cleveland
New Haven, Conn. • Waterville, Maine • London • Munich

On cover: Actors appear in a 1990 performance of
The Crucible at the National Theatre, London.

© 2003 by Lucent Books. Lucent Books is an imprint of The Gale Group, Inc.,
a division of Thomson Learning, Inc.

Lucent Books® and Thomson Learning™ are trademarks used herein under license.

For more information, contact
Lucent Books
27500 Drake Rd.
Farmington Hills, MI 48331-3535
Or you can visit our Internet site at http://www.gale.com

ALL RIGHTS RESERVED.
No part of this work covered by the copyright hereon may be reproduced or used in any form or
by any means—graphic, electronic, or mechanical, including photocopying, recording, taping,
Web distribution or information storage retrieval systems—without the written permission of the
publisher.

LIBRARY OF CONGRESS CATALOGING-IN-PUBLICATION DATA

Jimerson, M.N.
    Understanding *The Crucible* / by M.N. Jimerson.
    p. cm. — (Understanding great literature)
Summary: An introduction to Arthur Miller's play, *The Crucible*, discussing the author's
life, the impact of the play, its plot, cast of characters, literary criticism, and pertinence
for today's audiences.
Includes bibliographical references and index.
    ISBN 1-56006-996-1 (alk. paper)
    1. Miller, Arthur, 1915– Crucible—Juvenile literature. 2. Historical drama, American—
History and criticism—Juvenile literature. 3. Trials (Witchcraft) in literature—Juvenile
literature. 4. Salem (Mass.)—In literature—Juvenile literature. 5. Witchcraft in literature—Juvenile literature. [1. Miller, Arthur, 1915– Crucible. 2. American literature—
History and criticism.] I. Title. II. Series.
    PS3525.I5156C7344 2003
    812' .52—dc21
                                                                                    2002152878

Printed in the United States of America

Contents

FOREWORD

"Except for a living man, there is nothing more wonderful than a book!" wrote the widely respected nineteenth-century teacher and writer Charles Kingsley. A book, he continued, "is a message to us from human souls we never saw. And yet these [books] arouse us, terrify us, teach us, comfort us, open our hearts to us as brothers." There are many different kinds of books, of course; and Kingsley was referring mainly to those containing literature—novels, plays, short stories, poems, and so on. In particular, he had in mind those works of literature that were and remain widely popular with readers of all ages and from many walks of life.

Such popularity might be based on one or several factors. On the one hand, a book might be read and studied by people in generation after generation because it is a literary classic, with characters and themes of universal relevance and appeal. Homer's epic poems, the *Iliad* and the *Odyssey*, Chaucer's *Canterbury Tales*, Shakespeare's *Hamlet* and *Romeo and Juliet*, and Dickens's *A Christmas Carol* fall into this category. Some popular books, on the other hand, are more controversial. Mark Twain's *Huckleberry Finn* and J. D. Salinger's *The Catcher in the Rye*, for instance, have their legions of devoted fans who see them as great literature; while others view them as less than worthy because of their racial depictions, profanity, or other factors.

Still another category of popular literature includes realistic modern fiction, including novels such as Robert Cormier's *I Am the Cheese* and S. E. Hinton's *The Outsiders*. Their keen social insights and sharp character portrayals have consistently reached out to and captured the imaginations of many teenagers and young adults; and for this reason they are often assigned and studied in schools.

These and other similar works have become the "old standards" of the literary scene. They are the ones that people most often read, discuss, and study; and each has, by virtue of its content, critical success, or just plain longevity, earned the right to be the subject of a book examining its content. (Some, of course, like the *Iliad* and *Hamlet*, have been the subjects of numerous books already; but their literary stature is so lofty that there can never be too many books about them!) For millions of readers and students in one generation after another, each of these works becomes, in a sense, an adventure in appreciation, enjoyment, and learning.

The main purpose of Lucent's Understanding Great Literature series is to aid the reader in that ongoing literary adventure. Each volume in the series focuses on a single literary work that a majority of critics and teachers view as a classic and/or that is widely studied and discussed in schools. A typical volume first tells why the work in question is important. Then follow detailed overviews of the author's life, the work's historical background, its plot, its characters, and its themes. Numerous quotes from the work, as well as by critics and other experts, are interspersed throughout and carefully documented with footnotes for those who wish to pursue further research. Also included is a list of ideas for essays and other student projects relating to the work, an appendix of literary criticisms and analyses by noted scholars, and a comprehensive annotated bibliography.

The great nineteenth-century American poet Henry David Thoreau once quipped: "Read the best books first, or you may not have a chance to read them at all." For those who are reading or about to read the "best books" in the literary canon, the comprehensive, thorough, and thoughtful volumes of the Understanding Great Literature series are indispensable guides and sources of enrichment.

A Play for All Times

Arthur Miller believes that it is possible to make the world a better place. His conviction has carried him through a writing career of almost sixty-five years. In that time he has not only earned a place among America's greatest playwrights but transformed the American theater. Traditionally, serious drama concerns powerful or extraordinary people and great themes. Miller's work does involve great themes—human nature, the place of the individual in society, guilt, and betrayal—but his characters are ordinary people struggling under difficult circumstances.

The Crucible, too, is a play about ordinary people in a difficult situation, but Miller, who was known for his modern, urban settings, surprised everyone when he set *The Crucible* in 1692 Salem, Massachusetts. When the play opened in 1953, it received mixed reactions; some people loved it, others hated it. What is interesting is why it received such strong responses. The reactions stemmed not only from the play itself but also the political times in which Miller wrote it. People understood that *The Crucible* was about both 1690s America and 1950s America.

In seventeenth-century New England, witch-hunts were a fact of life. In an era of superstition and deep religious conviction, people believed that the devil and witches existed among them and that it was the individual's duty to seek out evildoers before evil could spread and destroy the whole community. From today's perspective it is clear that witch-hunters were mistaken, and historians have shown that witch-hunts were motivated by envy, fear, ambition, greed, repressive social rules, and even food poisoning.

Far removed from the Red Scare of the 1950s, and the even more recent disintegration of the Soviet Union, audiences today also see more in *The Crucible* than a fable about postwar America. But in 1953 a nervous public saw only the connection between Miller's tale and the hunt for Communists going on at the time. They were reluctant to praise the play in case they were labeled Communists. Later, people realized that *The Crucible* shows the damaging potential of repression in any place or time, not just 1692 or 1953 America. And since then it has become one of Arthur Miller's most-produced plays.

More than a political message makes *The Crucible* popular, however. Usually, audiences respond less to broad political debate than to personal and emotional struggle. The characters in *The Crucible* struggle. They struggle with each other and with their own consciences, with fear and with public opinion, with anger and revenge, with the urge to do right and the urge to right wrongs. In short, *The Crucible* is about people trying to live with other people. This is something everyone has to do, which makes the play interesting to everyone. Political times may change, but human nature does not. As long as this is true, *The Crucible's* popularity may endure.

The National Theatre of London performs Arthur Miller's play
The Crucible *in 1990.*

9

Life Imitating Art

The Crucible not only inspires audiences, it also influenced its author. In 1956 Miller testified before the House Un-American Activities Committee (HUAC) about writers' meetings he had attended that were organized by Communists. HUAC was well known for its single-minded search for those suspected of potentially subversive activity in American society. It considered Communists to be possible threats to national security and wanted Miller to name people who might be Communists. Miller refused, just as his character John Proctor in *The Crucible* refused to identify witches. It was a case of life imitating art and a demonstration of the power and influence stories can have in the real world.

Miller's Legacy

Few playwrights have managed to interweave life and art like Arthur Miller. He bases his plays on his life experiences and tries to live up to the ideals he explores in his art. His major theme is the struggle of the individual in society. Other recurring themes—responsibility to oneself and to others, memory of the past and its effect on the present, justice and the law—are all connected to that first theme. Since his dramas center on ordinary people, perhaps it is not surprising that Miller is credited with making serious drama popular. He also takes chances that broaden our understanding of what drama can be and make audiences more receptive to what new generations of playwrights might have to say.

Writer Ralph Ellison gave this tribute to Miller on the occasion of Miller's seventy-fifth birthday:

> Through your art you affirm the democratic vision by . . . making visible the marvelous diversity of the human condition. And by giving voice to the voiceless you provide perception to all those who have the heart and courage to see. In other words, you've been an eloquent explorer of America's turbulent and ever-shifting social hierarchy, and by reducing its chaos to artistic form you've given us a crucial gift of national self-consciousness. That I consider a marvelous achievement.[1]

CHAPTER ONE

Biography of Arthur Miller

Arthur Asher Miller was born in New York City on October 17, 1915. His parents, Isidore and Augusta, had three children, Kermit, Arthur, and Joan. In those early days no one imagined the future in store for the boy who seemed to love sports more than reading or writing.

The Miller children had a comfortable childhood. Isidore, a Jewish Austrian immigrant, owned a women's clothing store and put his energy into building up the family business. Augusta, born in New York of immigrant parents, was a former teacher who loved books and music. Though he did not know it, through his parents Arthur quietly absorbed an appreciation for the arts and for the value of hard work that would serve him in his future career.

Hard Times for the Miller Family: The Great Depression

The year Arthur turned fourteen, his world turned upside down. The Great Depression, a decade-long economic crash, began with the collapse of the New York Stock Market in 1929. Overnight, life became a struggle for survival for millions of people. Miller's family was affected too by this national calamity. Isidore's business failed, leaving little reason for the family to stay in the city. Since Augusta had relatives living in Brooklyn, the family moved there.

Isidore was discouraged by the failure of his business, and to Arthur's dismay it seemed his father simply gave up. As a child, Miller later wrote, he believed that "with sufficient intelligence a person could outwit the situation."[2] With maturity came his realization that events in the outside world can intrude without warning on one's private life and change its course, an insight that informs much of his work, including *The Crucible*.

Somehow the Millers got by as the depression worsened, and in 1932 Arthur graduated from high school. He applied for admission to the University of Michigan, but his grades in high school were not high enough to earn him a place there. Disappointed, Arthur looked for work and eventually took a job as a stock clerk. He also became a serious reader of literature by acknowledged masters such as Russian writer Fyodor Dostoyevsky. Each week he saved as much money as he could from his job and daydreamed about becoming a writer.

Birth of a Playwright: Miller at the University of Michigan

In 1934 Arthur applied again to the University of Michigan, setting out to convince admissions officers that he was ready for college and hungry to learn. Persistence paid off and he was accepted on trial as a journalism major. Journalism attracted him in part, he writes, because it was "a real profession with a boss and salary"[3]

Crowds throng the streets in front of the New York Stock Exchange. The stock market crash of 1929 set the stage for the Great Depression.

which would please his father. Had he followed this conventional path, perhaps he would have ended up as a reporter and the world would never have discovered one of its great playwrights. However, in his sophomore year Arthur heard about the annual Avery Hopwood Award for writing by students. In one week he wrote and submitted a play about a Jewish family in New York, called *No Villain*. Miller recalls: "On the day my name was called out before the assembled contestants and their guests as a Hopwood winner . . . I felt pleasure . . . but also . . . embarrassment, praying that everybody would soon forget my . . . play in favor of my next one, which would surely be better."[4]

Despite his embarrassment, Miller had received a valuable gift to a writer: encouragement. He began attending writing classes and switched majors from journalism to English. The next year, he won the Hopwood again for his second play, *Honors at Dawn*. He had also rewritten his first play, which under its new name *They Too Arise* won the Theatre Guild Bureau of New Plays Award and was staged in Ann Arbor and Detroit.

The Playwright Hones His Craft

When he graduated in 1938, Miller had completed a third play, *The Great Disobedience*, and chosen to pursue a writing career. He believed that "art ought to be of use in changing society."[5] He dreamed of seeing his plays produced on Broadway, but first he had an apprenticeship to serve.

He joined the Federal Theatre Project, where he cowrote a comedy called *Listen My Children* with another Michigan graduate, Norman Rosten. The Federal Theatre Project was a government-funded program founded in 1935 and designed to put actors and writers back to work during the depression. It was one of many New Deal programs created by the Democratic administration of Franklin D. Roosevelt to boost the American economy, but rumors began to circulate that this organization in particular had Communist ties. The newly formed House Un-American Activities Committee (HUAC) advised Congress to withdraw its financial support and the project was dismantled in 1939. Later, as a successful playwright, Miller would become all too familiar with HUAC and its anti-Communist investigations. But in 1939 his primary concerns were establishing himself as a writer and earning a living.

For the next five years, during World War II, Miller took a series of jobs and made time to write. In 1940 he married Mary Grace Slattery, whom he had met in college at Michigan. The couple settled in Brooklyn Heights and had two children, Jane and Robert. Miller wrote plays for radio, but while he appreciated the income and the opportunity to sharpen his playwriting skills, he disliked the restrictions placed on him by advertisers. Miller writes, "Rejected for military service, I . . . tried to justify my existence by throwing myself into writing patriotic war plays for radio . . . but the more expert I became the more dessicated [dried up] I felt writing the stuff, which was more like a form of yelling than writing. . . . Still, it . . . allowed me to continue working at plays and stories."[6]

In 1944 Miller wrote a play about a businessman called *The Man Who Had All the Luck*. It was published in a collection called *Cross-Section*, after which Herbert H. Harris agreed to produce it. Miller had written it as a serious drama about luck, success, and failure. Director Joseph Field, however, saw it as a comedy and staged it accordingly. It opened on Broadway in November but folded after only a few performances. As critic Neil Carson reveals, several flaws contributed to the play's failure on the stage:

A major problem . . . had been the time-consuming set changes necessitated by the script. Miller had called for four . . . realistic locations including a mechanic's shop with a car on stage. . . . Because all of the action was shown, there was very little emphasis on events before the curtain went up, and less exploration of the relationship between past actions and present consequences.

Although Miller worked a series of jobs in his twenties, he always found time to write.

Indeed . . . cause and effect was subverted [weakened] . . . because of Miller's . . . heavy reliance on coincidence. The result is that there is little attention paid to the relationship between man and society.[7]

Success! *All My Sons* and *Death of a Salesman*

The Man Who Had All the Luck received bad reviews, but their sting was lessened when the play won Miller another Theatre Guild Award. Miller learned a great deal from his first Broadway production: His later plays are more tightly structured, with less reliance on coincidence and clearer cause and effect relationships. Miller also strengthened his focus on the relationship between individuals and society in his later plays.

Over the next few years, Miller experimented successfully with other writing forms. He wrote a book based on interviews with American soldiers called *Situation Normal*, and a novel called *Focus* about anti-Semitism. But drama remained his primary literary form. With improved technique came his greatest success yet. *All My Sons* is the story of a man who indirectly causes the death of World War II pilots by knowingly selling faulty airplane parts to the government for profit. The play highlighted themes that were to reappear in *The Crucible*, such as individual responsibility, guilt and dishonesty, and the straining of family bonds. It opened in 1947, ran for more than three hundred performances, and won the New York Drama Critics Circle Award. In 1948 it was made into a motion picture.

Financially secure for the first time, Miller bought a farm in Connecticut, built a writing cabin, and began his next play. Several months later he sent the completed manuscript to producer Walter Fried. Fried liked it, hired respected stage director Elia Kazan, and soon the play, *Death of a Salesman*, was in rehearsal. In January 1949 it opened in Philadelphia, and in February it moved to Broadway.

Miller had already satisfied two dreams: He had become a writer, and he had reached Broadway. He had won awards and enjoyed financial success. *Death of a Salesman*, however, brought Miller international celebrity and cemented his reputation as a leading American playwright. The original production ran for 742 performances and the play won the 1949 Pulitzer Prize.

The original Broadway production of Miller's Death of a Salesman *in 1949 brought the playwright international acclaim.*

Death of a Salesman is the tale of Willy Loman, a traveling salesman who falls on hard times, becomes depressed, and loses his lifelong job. The play suggests that Willy's bitterness and unhappiness is caused by his faith in the American dream of success and his sense of failure when the dream does not come true for him.

No Longer a Private Citizen

With the enormous success of *Death of a Salesman*, Miller was no longer just a private citizen. He was a public figure who had become famous for communicating ideas vividly. Audiences drawn at first to his plays now paid attention to his personal and political views. Soon government officials were paying attention, too, and in the nation's climate of fear and suspicion, they were disturbed by what they heard. Critic Neil Carson writes, "As one of the New York stage's most exciting new talents, Miller found himself drawn more into the . . . spotlight. There his outspoken opposition to political persecution and his sympathy for leftist causes brought him . . . the unwelcome attention of the House Committee on Un-American Activities."[8]

Formed in 1938 to discover what influence Communists had in the United States, HUAC was led by demagogic Wisconsin senator Joseph McCarthy. The committee pressured people to testify before them and name Communists and Communist sympathizers. Those who refused might be found in contempt of Congress and even sent to jail. They could also be blacklisted—unofficially shunned by employers—effectively ruining their careers. In 1950 HUAC began investigating Hollywood and its related communities of writers, actors, and directors.

Miller's plays *All My Sons* and *Death of a Salesman* paint a less-than-flattering picture of capitalism and the American dream, implying that it is the source of much unhappiness. To HUAC officials this may have suggested the playwright had Communist sympathies. Idealistic and energetic, Miller's personal experiences during the depression had led him to question the way society worked. He was drawn to Socialist organizations, and became more involved in them as his success grew, including attending some Communist writers' meetings. In 1952 Miller's friend and director Elia Kazan testified before HUAC and named Miller as a Socialist sympathizer.

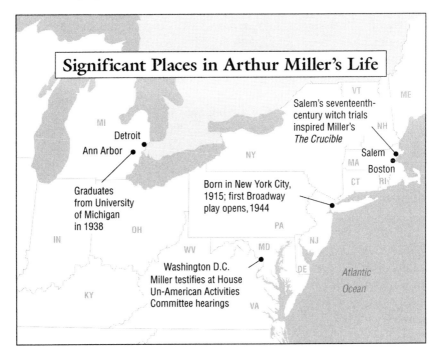

Significant Places in Arthur Miller's Life

Salem's seventeenth-century witch trials inspired Miller's *The Crucible*

Detroit

Ann Arbor

Graduates from University of Michigan in 1938

Born in New York City, 1915; first Broadway play opens, 1944

Salem

Boston

Washington D.C. Miller testifies at House Un-American Activities Committee hearings

Atlantic Ocean

This would have hardened HUAC's suspicions of Miller, but Miller's next play, *The Crucible*, suggests he was just as suspicious of HUAC and its influence on American culture and politics. He objected to the tactics employed by the committee. Their trials, and the mood of fear and suspicion they engendered in America reminded him of another time in American history when mass hysteria led to public persecutions: 1692, when a witch-hunt led to the hanging of nineteen people in Salem, Massachusetts.

When *The Crucible* opened on Broadway on January 22, 1953, Miller's analogies were not hard to see. Some people thought he had gone beyond a portrayal of the failure of justice to a potentially subversive condemnation of the American government motivated by Socialist sympathies.

The negative effects at first were limited to a few unfavorable reviews which suggest *The Crucible* is not as good as *Death of a Salesman*. More aggressive reviews followed suggesting Miller's allegory had failed because witches do not exist but Communists do. Ultimately, the play had only moderate success, closing after 197 performances, although it did win the Antoinette Perry and Donaldson Awards for best drama of 1953.

After the unsympathetic reviews and modest run of *The Crucible* came other setbacks. Miller applied for a passport in order to attend a European premier of *The Crucible* in Brussels, Belgium, only to have his application denied as against national interests in light of ongoing HUAC hearings. The two one-act plays he completed in 1955, *A View from the Bridge* and *A Memory of Two Mondays*, ran for only 149 performances. Then a film project about gangs that he was working on for the Youth Board in New York City was canceled when some groups opposed the use of public money to fund writing by a Socialist sympathizer. Miller was beginning to experience the downside of fame.

Miller Under Attack

Miller's celebrity also put a strain on his marriage to Mary Slattery, which had begun to break down by 1951. In 1955 he began a relationship with film actress Marilyn Monroe, one of the most famous women in the world. Monroe had met Miller in 1950, introduced by Elia Kazan, but the relationship became more serious after she divorced renowned baseball player Joe DiMaggio and

Miller's delight is evident as he dances with his famous wife, Marilyn Monroe.

moved to New York in the spring of 1955. Rumors about the couple began circulating; in June 1956 Miller divorced Slattery and married Monroe a couple of weeks later.

The romance between a famous intellectual playwright and a glamorous film star captured the public imagination, particularly since Monroe was beautiful, hugely popular, and had already been married to baseball icon DiMaggio. HUAC, which had been losing support since the discrediting of McCarthy in 1954, saw perhaps an opportunity to garner some publicity for its cause. In the spring of 1956 HUAC subpoenaed Miller to testify, ostensibly about the misuse of passports but actually to investigate Miller's Communist sympathies, if any, and his attacks on HUAC.

Miller answered HUAC's questions about his past, and denied ever belonging to the Communist Party. But he refused to name people who had attended Communist writers' meetings with him, much like John Proctor in *The Crucible* refuses to identify witches. In 1957 Miller was found guilty of contempt, fined, and given a one-month suspended sentence. A year later, the sentence was overturned on appeal, in part perhaps because public sympathy lay with Miller and his popular wife.

Trouble at Home

With the wane of HUAC's influence, Miller was once again respected and employable. He and Monroe flew to London, England, where filming began on *The Prince and the Showgirl*, starring Monroe and respected British actor Laurence Olivier. Miller rewrote *A View from the Bridge*, which opened at London's Comedy Theatre that fall. He also wrote a story called *The Misfits*. But he wrote little else. Most of his time was spent taking care of his wife, whose dependance on drugs, alcohol, and constant emotional support was becoming increasingly problematic. Monroe's first pregnancy had ended in miscarriage in August 1956, and the actress was prone to deep depression. Miller encouraged her to work; she completed *Some Like It Hot* in November 1958, and he promised to adapt *The Misfits* into a screenplay for her. But the marriage was further strained by a second miscarriage in December 1958, the couple's opposing lifestyles, Monroe's romantic relationship with actor Yves Montand during the shooting of *Let's Make Love,* and the fact that the couple lived under intense media scrutiny. By the time filming began on *The Misfits* in July 1960 the marriage was over, and in January 1961 Monroe and Miller were divorced.

After the Fall

In 1961, following Miller's divorce from Monroe and the death of his mother, the playwright moved back to Connecticut, exhausted and depressed. In 1962 he began work on a new play, *After the Fall,* to be directed by Elia Kazan. Though the two men had been estranged after Kazan's cooperation with HUAC, time had eased the strain on their friendship. As always, Miller drew from life experiences for his writing; *After the Fall* is a semiautobiographical work about a writer's troubled personal and professional relationships.

During writing, he became involved with photographer Inge Morath, whom he had met on the set of *The Misfits*. Miller and Morath were married in 1962, and their daughter, Rebecca, was born in 1963. A few months after their marriage, Marilyn Monroe died in Los Angeles by accidental drug overdose. Miller avoided the press as far as possible during the sensational media blitz surrounding the star's death and continued work on *After the Fall*. Rehearsals began in 1963, and the play opened in 1964, but audience reaction and critical reviews were negative. Miller was accused of exploiting his relationship with the late Monroe and criticized for airing the couple's private disagreements in public in order to justify himself.

Miller went back to work on a new play, *Incident at Vichy*, which addresses anti-Semitism. This play, which also opened in 1964, received a more positive response. Overseas his work was often in production, which led Miller to spend a good part of his time in Europe. One such notable production was Laurence Olivier's staging of *The Crucible* at Britain's National Theatre in 1965. *A View from the Bridge* was successfully revived off-Broadway that same year.

Speaking Out for Free Speech

Also in 1965 came a staging in Paris of *After the Fall*, so Miller arranged a trip to France. While there, he received an unexpected invitation. David Carver, secretary general of the international literary organization PEN (Poets, Playwrights, Editors, Essayists, and Novelists), asked him if he would consider becoming the society's president. Though at the time Miller was unfamiliar with PEN, the organization admired Miller and his writing and felt the playwright would be the ideal person to represent the group in its work advocating for free speech for writers living under any political system of government. Miller had always been politically outspoken, and his principled stand against HUAC during the 1950s had earned the respect and trust of writers throughout the world. More than most, he had demonstrated the close connection between his life and his art, as well as his belief that writing ought to serve society in some way. Miller accepted the appointment, and the presidency

Miller married photographer Inge Morath in 1962.

21

Miller served as a delegate to the 1968 Democratic Convention. He appears here on the convention floor with Paul Newman, the actor.

of PEN marked a new phase in his career as political activist. He used his position as a well-known and respected playwright to campaign on behalf of all writers targeted by their governments for expressing dissenting political views. Miller went on to serve a second term, heading PEN until 1969 when he retired from the post.

The 1960s also saw Miller become increasingly involved in mainstream politics. Prompted by the escalation in social unrest and injustice that he saw around him, Miller attended the 1968 National Democratic Convention as a delegate. He was strongly opposed to the conflict in Vietnam but his resolution at the convention that the United States stop the bombing was rejected. Though discouraged by what he saw as a collapse of social and political ethics, Miller continued to write, convinced that ultimately the public needed hope that the future could be better.

Professionally, Miller's reputation as one of America's great playwrights remained secure. In 1966 *Death of a Salesman* was broadcast on television, followed in 1967 by *The Crucible*. Seen against the backdrop of the Vietnam War and the antiwar movement, it at last became clear to a wider audience that *The Crucible* is about more than Salem or McCarthyism, and the play's exploration of individual conscience took on fresh relevance and popularity. The playwright continued to produce new work including *The Price* in 1968, which despite hitches during rehearsal, ran for 425 performances in New York and a further year in London, England. He also explored other literary forms. In 1967 he published a collection of short stories called *I Don't Need You Any More*, and in 1969 he wrote a travel journal called *In Russia*, illustrated with photographs by his wife Inge, in which he shares his perceptions of Russian society and people.

The Soviet Union banned Miller's work in 1970, displeased with the playwright's determination to campaign on behalf of dissident writers. Undeterred, Miller continued his involvement in politics and attended a second Democratic National Convention as delegate, this time in 1972 in Miami. On the whole, Miller found his new work underappreciated in the United States during the 1970s. American critics did not respond favorably to his 1972 *The Creation of the World and Other Business*, surprised by Miller's departure from the realism that had previously been a hallmark of his work. Miller started work on *The American Clock*, inspired by Studs Terkel's book *Hard Times: An Oral History of the Depression*. But the playwright was dissatisfied with the script. He set it aside until 1974, when director Dan Sullivan presented a reading of the play by the Seattle Repertory Company that encouraged Miller to revisit it. That same year, *The Creation of the World* was rewritten as a musical called *Up from Paradise* and premiered at Miller's alma mater, the University of Michigan.

The Archbishop's Ceiling, inspired by Miller's 1969 visit to Prague, Czechoslovakia, fared poorly when it opened in Washington, D.C., in 1977. Then, in 1979 Miller's play *The Price* was revived in Charleston, South Carolina, before moving to Broadway. Miller decided to present *The American Clock* to the public in the same way. But although the play was successful in Charleston, it ran for only twelve performances on Broadway after poor reviews.

Miller did have several successful New York revivals of his work in the 1970s, including *The Crucible* in 1972 and *Death of a Salesman* in 1975. But his literary output was not limited to new and revived plays. He published a second travel journal with Morath,

In the Country, in 1977 and a compilation of his theater essays in 1978. He also visited China, which led to his 1979 travel journal *Chinese Encounters*, again illustrated with his wife's photographs.

Four years later Miller directed *Death of a Salesman* in Beijing with a Chinese cast, and a journal followed in 1984 called *Salesman in Beijing*. The journal documents the challenges of presenting a play defining one culture to audiences from a different culture. Once again, Miller's example demonstrates how literature based on universal themes can cross national boundaries and speak to people from diverse backgrounds. This truism was further illustrated when audiences in London, England, received both *The American Clock* and *The Archbishop's Ceiling* enthusiastically in the 1980s, the plays at last coming into their own despite their lackluster reception in the United States in the 1970s.

The 1980s on the whole upheld Miller's reputation as one of America's greatest playwrights. *A View from the Bridge* reappeared on Broadway in 1983. *Death of a Salesman* was revived

Miller (standing, center) is among those honored for lifetime achievement by the Kennedy Center in 1984.

there in 1984 with Dustin Hoffman as Willy Loman. That same year Miller was honored by the Kennedy Center with an award for lifetime achievement. The ceremony was held in the same room in which the playwright's patriotism had been questioned by HUAC during the 1950s. In a further vindication of Miller, the CBS television network broadcast *Death of a Salesman* in 1985 with Dustin Hoffman reprising his role as Willy. The play aired to an estimated audience of 25 million people. The following year, *The Crucible* was revived in New York and Washington, D.C.

Miller had been producing new plays too in the 1980s. The one-act plays *Elegy for a Lady* and *Some Kind of Love Story* were produced in 1982 under the title *2 by A.M. in Connecticut* and published two years later under the title *Two-Way Mirror*. Another pair of one-acts, *I Can't Remember Anything* and *Clara* were produced under the title *Danger: Memory!* in 1987. That same year Miller published a well-received autobiography, *Timebends: A Life*. It sets his personal experiences against the background of their political times. In a departure from the traditional biography form, Miller also switches back and forth in time instead of simply starting with childhood and working through time year by year. In this way, the author links memories separated by time but joined in meaning: the way people really remember things.

The 1990s opened with a film version of *Some Kind of Love Story* called *Everybody Wins*. PBS broadcast a production of *An Enemy of the People* in 1990, and *Clara* was presented on television in 1991. That year Miller received a Mellon Bank Award for lifetime achievement in the humanities and was the subject of *The South Bank Show*—a respected long-running English television series known for its in-depth examinations of artists and culture. The playwright continued to offer up new work including *The Last Yankee* and *The Ride Down Mt. Morgan* in 1991 and *Broken Glass* in 1994, three plays that explore marriage relationships. *Mr. Peter's Connections* premiered in 1998, featuring an elderly man's examination of his life and family relationships.

Miller earned further accolades mid-decade, receiving the William Inge Festival Award for distinguished achievement in American theater in 1995. This year marked the playwright's eightieth birthday, marked by celebrations in both the United States and England. In 1996 Miller received the Edward Albee

Miller attends a rehearsal of one of his plays. Although Miller's recent work has met with only moderate success, his place as one of America's premier playwrights is assured.

Last Frontier Playwright Award and a revised and expanded version of his *Theater Essays* was published, edited by respected Miller critic Steven R. Centola.

Although Miller has not enjoyed significant success yet with his more recent plays, the 1990s are notable for the film version of *The Crucible*. Miller himself wrote the screenplay for this successful 1996 adaptation directed by Nicholas Hytner and featuring Daniel Day-Lewis as John Proctor, Winona Ryder as Abigail Williams, and Paul Scofield as Deputy-Governor Danforth. Day-Lewis met Miller's daughter Rebecca during shooting, and the two later married.

In 1998 Miller's play *A View from the Bridge* was revived, going on to win two Tony Awards, and a revised version of *The Ride Down Mt. Morgan* was produced on Broadway. The following year saw the fiftieth anniversary of *Death of a Salesman*. To mark the occasion, the play was revived in New York and won the 1999 Tony for best revival.

In the new century came renewed interest in Miller's work. Both *The Ride Down Mt. Morgan* and *The Price* reappeared in New York in 2000, a year which marked Miller's eighty-fifth birthday.

Miller's alma mater, the University of Michigan, hosted a celebration. So too did the Arthur Miller Centre for American Studies established in 1987 at the University of East Anglia in Norwich, England. *Echoes Down the Corridor*, a collection of Miller's essays from 1944 to 2000, was published that year too.

In 2001 Miller was awarded a fellowship from the National Endowment for the Humanities as well as the John H. Finley Award for Exemplary Service to New York City. In the same year, *The Man Who Had All the Luck* was revived at the Williamstown Theatre Festival, and a film was made of his novel *Focus*. In 2002 the Roundabout Theatre Company revived *The Man Who Had All the Luck*, and that same year a successful revival of *The Crucible* opened on Broadway. Scheduled for a limited engagement, it opened on March 7 and ran for 120 performances to packed houses. The revival, directed by Richard Eyre, featured stars Liam Neeson as John Proctor and Laura Linney as his wife, Elizabeth. But 2002 was also a year of sadness for Miller. Inge Morath, his wife of forty years, to whom he dedicated *Timebends*, died in January of lymphatic cancer.

"Creating a New Shadow on the Earth"

In *Timebends*, Miller recounts a memory. Fifteen years old, he bought lumber and built a new porch for the family home on Third Street in Brooklyn. Years later, he built a cabin near his home in Connecticut, a place where he could "write a play about a salesman." For Miller the two building projects were linked by a feeling of accomplishment and pleasure. For him "the idea of creating a new shadow on the earth . . . never lost its fascination."[9] The creative urge has been expressed in Miller's drama ever since.

In the United States, the Arthur Miller Society is dedicated to the study of Miller's work. Miller has proven to be a playwright of idealism, integrity, clear vision, and determination, who lives what he writes, acts on his convictions, and speaks plainly. Fellow playwright David Hare sums it up, "The best thing I ever heard Arthur Miller say was . . . when [an] . . . interviewer . . . asked him whether it hadn't needed extraordinary courage to defy the House Un-American Activities Committee. 'Not at all,' said Miller. 'After everything I'd written, if I hadn't defied them, I would have looked a complete idiot.'"[10]

CHAPTER TWO

Historical Background

The Crucible is not history; it is a play based on historical events in 1692 Salem. Miller used some facts, rearranged others, and produced the play from his imagination. The result is a story that draws audiences in and makes them think—about the past and the present, about human nature, and about themselves.

Miller dramatizes the witch-hunts of seventeenth-century Salem in *The Crucible*, revealing their similarities to the Communist-hunts of the 1950s which were taking place as he wrote. Both periods in America were characterized by widespread paranoia and the belief that loyal citizens should protect their government from potential subversives by informing on one another. Suspects were ruthlessly pursued and encouraged to confess and expose others in order to save themselves.

Seventeenth-Century Salem

The Puritans who founded the Massachusetts Bay Colony obtained their charter from King Charles I in 1629. The Massachusetts Bay Company was to be a trading venture with headquarters in England, but Puritans in the company bought out their partners and emigrated to the colony. They wanted to retain control of the company, escape further religious persecution in England, and establish a god-fearing community of saints who would set an example of righteousness to the world.

Governor Winthrop's words to the arriving pilgrims established the colonists' philosophy: "We must not look only on our own things, but also on the things of our brethren."[11] Historians Paul Boyer and Stephen Nissenbaum describe Winthrop's plan: "the constant scrutiny and regulation of all facets of individual behavior in order to nip in the bud deviations that threatened the interests of the community as a whole."[12]

Puritans believed a chosen few were predestined for heaven, and these select were saints eligible for election to Puritan churches. Intolerant of anything that threatened their beliefs, they banned other religions, hanging Quakers whose spiritual beliefs contradicted theirs. In their minds witches also posed a threat. Puritans brought the two-hundred-year-old European tradition of witch-hunting to America. They believed witches contracted with the devil by signing his book, and maliciously caused the ills that befell their communities. Witches were tried and convicted based on hearsay, the testimony of other accused witches, and the presence of birthmarks with which they allegedly suckled evil animal companions called familiars. They were tortured until they confessed and then were hanged. Antiwitch paranoia suffused the colony, and Salem Village sermons were of the hellfire and damnation variety that forbade independent thinking and inspired fear and guilt. Historian Edmund S. Morgan explains, members "guarded each other's morals by censuring or excommunicating . . . those who strayed."[13]

Salem expert Frances Hill reveals that Salem Village, now modern-day Danvers, where the witch-hunts took place, was initially a farm community established to provide food for prosperous, sophisticated Salem Town, a two-to three-hour walk away. Over time, the farmers began to resent the town's control of village affairs; because of town opposition, the village did not even have its own official church until 1689 when Reverend Samuel Parris was ordained. Historians Paul Boyer and Stephen Nissenbaum also suggest that the town's focus on trade rather than God "represented a . . . *moral* threat."[14] The splitting of the village into factions added to the stress of living there. Envy played its part too. The educated, wealthy inhabitants of Salem Town outshone the farmers of Salem Village, and prospering newcomers to the village were resented by older elite village families like the Putnams who saw their own properties subdivided with each generation.

Salem was split along gender lines too. Women had little power and unwed girls lacked status. Puritan tradition branded women as sinners who inherited sin from Eve and passed it on through childbirth.

A fanciful illustration captures the air of drama that pervaded the Salem witch trials.

Witch-hunting guides of the time reveal an alarming degree of woman-hatred and would have been familiar to inquisitors and judges. More women than men were accused of witchcraft, and girls felt intense pressure to fulfill social expectations.

The Witch-Hunts

These tensions created extreme anxiety which finally erupted in January 1692 when Reverend Parris's nine-year-old daughter, Betty, and eleven-year-old niece, Abigail Williams, were seized by fits of shaking, screaming that demons were attacking them. Within a month the hysterical symptoms spread to other Salem girls. Parris consulted a doctor and, swayed by recent reports of witchcraft from Boston minister Cotton Mather, they decided the devil was to blame.

Parris also met with neighboring ministers John Hale of Beverly and bigoted Nicholas Noyes of Salem. They agreed that Satan was at work in Salem and advised patience. Parris did not want to wait, afraid he and his family might be accused of being the devil's tools rather than his victims. He beat his Caribbean Indian slave Tituba to force her to confess to witchcraft and pushed the girls to name their persecutors. They named Tituba, as well as poverty-stricken Sarah Good and ailing, aging Sarah Osborne, as witches. On February 29 the three were arrested, and on March 1 when they appeared before magistrates John Hathorne and Jonathan Corwin at the village meeting house, Tituba confessed.

Tituba, Good, and Osborne were sent to a Boston jail, but the girls continued to be afflicted. They blamed unlikely witches such as Good's four-year-old daughter Dorcas, pious Martha Corey, and esteemed Rebecca Nurse, who were jailed. In the weeks that followed, prayer and sermons by Parris and his friend from Boston, former village minister Reverend Deodat Lawson, failed to relieve the girls' fits. Instead more accusations followed, mostly of enemies of the Putnam clan. Hathorne and Corwin, the two Salem merchants serving as magistrates, were joined by the deputy governor of Massachusetts Thomas Danforth and Boston clergyman Samuel Sewall to hear the cases. That April, outspoken tavernkeeper John Proctor and his wife Elizabeth, Bridget Bishop, and quarrelsome old Giles Corey were among those imprisoned. In May, George Burroughs, a former minister of Salem and Putnam opponent, was arrested in Maine, brought to Salem to face charges of witchcraft, and later jailed. Sarah Osborne meanwhile died in prison.

In a 1954 stage production, townswomen angrily hurl accusations at each other.

That same month, Reverend Increase Mather, the renowned Boston minister, returned from England, bringing with him a new charter for the Royal Colony of Massachusetts and a new royal governor, Sir William Phipps. Beset on all sides by demands that he deal decisively with the witchcraft issue, Phipps set up a special court of oyer and terminer to quickly hear (oyer) and determine (terminer) the cases. He appointed as judges his lieutenant governor William Stoughton, Nathaniel Saltonstall, Bartholomew Gedney, Peter Sergeant, Samuel Sewall, Wait Still Winthrop, and John Richards, as well as the two magistrates already involved, Hathorne and Corwin.

In June, during the court's opening sessions, Bridget Bishop was the first to be found guilty and sentenced to death. The judges began with her case because twelve years earlier she had been accused of witchcraft. A suspected witch could be safely convicted with little public opposition. Trial methods included accepting spectral evidence—the supposition that the devil could take on the shape or specter of someone and in that form harm others. Such evidence was virtually impossible to challenge by the

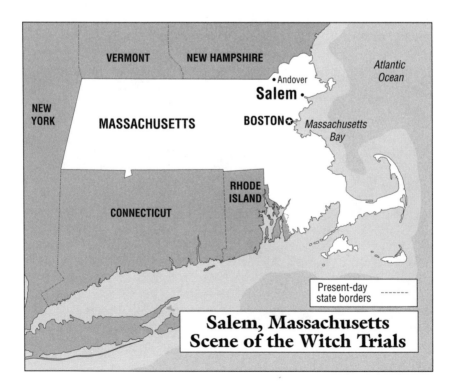

**Salem, Massachusetts
Scene of the Witch Trials**

defendants. Not long after this trial, Nathaniel Saltonstall resigned from the court unhappy with its conduct; he was later accused of witchcraft himself but never tried. Bishop, despite maintaining her innocence, was hanged. After that, the number of accusations multiplied though some questioned the verdicts. Toward the end of the month, Rebecca Nurse and Sarah Good were among those condemned to death. On July 19 Nurse was hanged even though friends had signed a petition on her behalf. By then the hysteria had spread to the nearby town of Andover.

August saw more trials, including those of the Proctors and Reverend George Burroughs. Elizabeth was spared death because she was pregnant, but the minister and John Proctor were hanged on August 19, and still the trials continued. Giles Corey was pressed to death, under large stones on September 19 for refusing to answer the accusations, and a few days later his wife Martha was hanged.

The End of the Witch-Hunt

By now, public opinion was greatly disturbed. Twenty people were dead, 150 were in jail, and another 200 faced accusations. Corruption was rampant, with marshals seizing the property of the convicted and selling it to line their pockets. Scarcely anyone was safe from the girls' accusations; charges had spread to include prominent citizens of Massachusetts—though many of the wealthy eluded trial or escaped from prison, bribing their way out of trouble. The supposedly bewitched girls had even accused magistrate Jonathan Corwin's mother-in-law, Reverend John Hale's wife, and Lady Phipps, wife of the new governor. But in doing so they went too far, and official opinion turned against them. Increase Mather, a renowned Boston minister and father of the zealous witch-hunter Cotton Mather, wrote a book called *Cases of Conscience Concerning Evil Spirits Personating Men*. In it he declared that to condemn one innocent person was worse than allowing ten guilty ones to escape. He cast doubts on the validity of spectral evidence, a sentiment shared by eminent Boston merchant Thomas Brattle who wrote a letter on October 8 in which he questioned the credibility of the witnesses and the prejudices of the judges. On October 12, at a meeting of the General Court of the colony, a worried Phipps banned additional imprisonments and declared that spectral evidence was no longer permissible. At the end of October he dissolved the court of oyer and terminer. A month later the General Court of the colony created the Massachusetts Superior

Boston minister Increase Mather condemned the Salem witch trials.

Court to hear the remaining cases. Since spectral evidence was no longer admissible, thirty cases were dismissed, twenty-six were tried, and three found guilty. Those three were found guilty only because two confessed who were not mentally competent and one confessed because her husband had been hung for retracting his confession. All were reprieved.

Historian Brian P. Levack sums up the witch trials: "The great majority of witches were old, poor women. . . . In the early stages . . . victims conformed to the stereotype, but as the hunts progressed a higher percentage of wealthy and powerful individuals . . . were named. . . . The breakdown of the stereotype . . . prompt[ed] . . . officials to . . . end . . . the trials. . . . Governor Phipps helped to end the Salem trials after his own wife had been accused. . . ."[15]

Fact or Fiction?

In *The Crucible* Miller altered some of the witch-trial facts for dramatic purposes. There was no dancing in the forest, Ruth Putnam's real name was Ann and she was not an only child, Tituba was of Indian not African descent, and there was no romantic relationship between Abigail Williams and John Proctor (the former being only eleven, and the latter in his sixties). Miller also merged some of the ministers, magistrates, and girls; for example it was Mercy, not Abigail, who saw her parents murdered. Miller was inspired by *The Devil in Massachusetts*, a book about the Salem witch trials written by Marion Starkey and published in 1949. According to journalist Frances Hill, Starkey's book unfortunately "frequently lapses into fiction."[16] While some facts were altered in Miller's play, the essential fact—that innocent people were executed—was not changed.

A New Witch-Hunt

Salem believed witches wished to overthrow the church and set up Satan in its place. Americans in the 1950s feared a Communist plot to topple the government. The House Un-American Activities Committee (HUAC), established in 1938 to uncover Communist influence in America, launched a series of investigations, promising immunity to those who named potential subversives. Some did so hoping to prove their loyalty and avoid trouble. Uncooperative witnesses lost their jobs and reputations. Miller critic Neil Carson explains,

> The real danger of [HUAC] was not its . . . purpose of searching out enemies of the state, but the extra-legal means it employed. . . . Since witnesses before the Committee hearings were not technically accused of anything, they were provided with none of the safeguards [that] protect witnesses in a court of law. . . . Hearsay, prejudice and allegation became part of the official record. Furthermore, far from protecting the identity of the witnesses, [HUAC] did all it could to publicise its hearings so that "unfriendly" witnesses could be exposed to an increasingly hysterical public opinion. Refusals to answer questions . . . were generally considered . . . admissions of guilt. . . . Innumerable careers were damaged or destroyed . . . and more than a dozen suicides have been linked to appearances, or subpoenas to appear, before [HUAC].[17]

The Reason for HUAC's Mistrust

During World War II America and the Soviet Union were united against Hitler. After the war their opposing political philosophies—capitalism and communism—triggered suspicion and a push for nuclear weapon superiority between the two world powers: a Cold War. The Soviet Union's aggressive takeover of its immediate neighbors and China's conversion to communism convinced many Americans that Communists would target the United States next. HUAC began investigating trade union members, writers, public employees such as teachers—anyone who might have influence over groups of people—to unearth Communists.

In 1950 ambitious Wisconsin senator Joseph McCarthy fanned the flames of national paranoia. He claimed President Truman's government was overrun by Communists and declared he had a list of their names. In the four years that followed, anti-Communist hysteria reached its peak in the United States as McCarthy targeted government employees, congressmen, and eventually, to his cost, even the army. Howard Zinn, a historian, describes the situation: "[Some senators] proposed . . . the setting up of detention centers . . . for suspected subversives, who, when the President declared an "internal security emergency," would be held without trial. . . . The proposed camps were set up ready for use."[18]

Several people were accused of spying for the Soviet Union, among them Julius and Ethel Rosenberg, who were found guilty and sentenced to death. Despite appeals to Presidents Truman and Eisenhower, the Rosenbergs were executed on June 19, 1953. Howard Zinn continues, "It was a demonstration to the people of the country . . . of what lay at the end of the line for those the government decided were traitors."[19] Ellen Schrecker suggests:

> Most victims of McCarthyism . . . were Communists, former Communists, or people who worked closely with Communists.

Senator Joseph McCarthy points to a map revealing the locations of alleged Communist organizations. McCarthy conducted a series of investigations to expose Communists within the government.

There were other cases—people whose names had gotten on the wrong mailing lists or who had the wrong kinds of friends—that . . . fed the . . . misperception that McCarthyism targeted ordinary individuals. It did not. Most of the thousands of Americans who suffered during the anti-Communist frenzy of the 1940s and 1950s were not "innocent" victims in the way that phrase was used at the time. They had been in or near the Communist party. The political repression directed against them was justified . . . under the prevailing assumption that as "Commies" they had no rights that deserved protection.[20]

Also, Paul Boyer and Stephen Nissenbaum point out that like Governor Winthrop two centuries earlier, HUAC felt "the care of the public must oversway all private respects."[21]

Miller and HUAC

When *The Crucible* opened in 1953 critics saw it as intentional, subversive criticism of McCarthy's investigations. Reception to the play was chilly on opening night and Miller recalls how acquaintances in the audience ignored him as they left the theater. Critics considered the play a failed allegory prompted by Miller's liberal bias; they pointed out that whereas witches do not, as far as they knew, exist, Communists do. *The Crucible* had a short run compared with that of Miller's greatest success, *Death of a Salesman*.

Death of a Salesman criticizes the American dream of material success; *The Crucible* presents a hero, John Proctor, who challenges the government by confronting its representative, Deputy Governor Danforth. In the prevailing climate of fear these messages were seen as dangerous, and Miller's career suffered as a result, even though he did not appear before HUAC until 1956. By that time McCarthy had been censured for abusing his power as senator and public anti-Communist hysteria was on the wane.

The Witch-Hunts Compared

Critics dismissed *The Crucible* claiming that no true comparison could be made between people accused of witchcraft—an imaginary crime—and those accused of being Communists, since Communists exist. But Miller's allegory is successful on levels beyond that comparison. In both hunts, to be accused was to be assumed guilty, to accuse was to avoid punishment. Confession and accusation were

*Miller testifies before HUAC in 1956. Many Americans felt that Miller
wrote* The Crucible *as a criticism of Senator McCarthy and HUAC.*

actively encouraged, the legal process was perverted or avoided in
order to secure convictions, and innocent people were destroyed.
Paranoia and hysteria characterized both periods, and many compro-
mised their values in order to survive. Political and social uncertainty
and repression was a feature of both eras, and unscrupulous individuals used the hunts to further their own ends. With *The Crucible*,
Miller successfully expresses the notion "that the sin of public terror
. . . divests man of conscience, of himself."[22]

CHAPTER THREE

The Plot

From its tense opening scene to its tragic conclusion, *The Crucible* traces a community's journey from unease to crisis. But to understand the escalation of events in Salem, it is helpful to briefly set the scene and outline some background events. The action takes place toward the end of the seventeenth century in Salem, a village in colonial Massachusetts. Salem was originally founded as a haven for Puritans who wanted to escape religious persecution in their former homeland of England. As a result, religion plays a significant role in this small farming community, and the battle between good and evil is as real to the villagers as the ongoing struggles with the Indians over land rights. Land and religion also came bitter disagreements between the villagers. Neighbors argue over boundaries. The village is divided in its support of Reverend Parris as Salem's minister. Salem's residents live in a constant state of stress stemming from fear of Indian attacks, superstition, and simmering resentments. Their anxiety is intensified by a repressive atmosphere that limits freedom of thought or action. This buildup of pressure partly explains how things could go so wrong so quickly in Salem.

Act 1: "Witchery's a Hangin' Error"

It is a spring day in 1692, and in Salem a young girl lies in her bed, seemingly unconscious. She is one of a group of girls caught dancing in the forest at night with a slave called Tituba. Salem's minister Reverend Samuel Parris discovered the dancers. The unconscious girl is his daughter Betty; Tituba is his Caribbean slave; and the girl who led the dancing is his niece Abigail Williams.

Parris is disturbed. He has been praying by Betty's bed since midnight. Doctor Griggs can find no medical reason for Betty's fit. Folk are gathering in the minister's home, whispering of witchcraft. Parris has sent for expert witch-hunter Reverend Hale of

In this scene from the 1996 film version of The Crucible, *Abigail (left) and Tituba dance in the woods.*

Beverly to investigate the matter. While waiting for Hale, Parris sternly questions his niece to uncover the truth before the rumors spread further. Parris's great fear is that his enemies will take this opportunity to declare him unfit to be minister.

Abigail denies that anything happened in the forest beyond dancing. Parris questions her about her reputation in the village and her inability to find employment. She accuses her former employer Elizabeth Proctor of spreading malicious lies about her. Thomas and Ann Putnam arrive and reveal that their daughter Ruth is afflicted just like Betty. Ann admits that she sent Ruth to Tituba to discover the identity of the witch she is convinced murdered her seven other children in infancy.

Parris is shocked to learn that the girls may have been practicing witchcraft after all. Thomas urges him to reveal all to the villagers but Parris wants to wait until Hale arrives. Just then the Putnams' servant Mercy Lewis appears with the news that Ruth seems a little better. Thomas convinces Parris to go downstairs and lead the villagers assembled there in psalm singing. When the Putnams and Parris depart, Abigail and Mercy discuss their forest activities. Mary Warren, another of the girls in the forest, arrives terrified. She wants Abigail to admit to dancing before all the girls are accused of the worse crime of witchcraft, for "witchery's a hangin' error."[23] Betty rouses, frightened. Abigail tells Betty she has nothing to fear since her father knows everything that happened in the forest, but Betty is still afraid. She calls for her dead mother and tries to fly out of the window. Abigail pulls her back and Betty cries out that Abigail did not admit to drinking blood as part of a spell to kill Elizabeth Proctor. Abigail threatens to kill any girl who admits to anything beyond dancing and Tituba's attempts to conjure dead spirits.

John Proctor appears at the door curious to learn the source of the commotion in the village. He is a farmer married to Elizabeth. Mary Warren is their maid and he orders her home. Betty is again seemingly unconscious, and Mary and Mercy leave Proctor and Abigail alone together. Abigail was the Proctors' maid until Elizabeth discovered John committing adultery with her and dismissed her. Abigail still loves John and sees Elizabeth as the obstacle between them. John finds Abigail attractive but considers their affair over. He does not know she wants Elizabeth dead. He cautions her to forget any hopes that their relationship will resume.

As they talk, Betty wakes up screaming. Apparently the psalms have disturbed her. People hurry into the room, including Rebecca Nurse, Reverend Parris, Giles Corey, and Thomas Putnam, all debating whether or not she is possessed. Rebecca stands by Betty and soon the child is

Abigail is in love with John Proctor, and she schemes to get rid of his wife, Elizabeth.

41

In this movie still, Salem's teenage girls make terrified accusations of witchcraft.

calm. Rebecca doubts witchcraft caused the fit. She blames it on the silliness of young girls. But apart from Proctor, the others are not convinced. During the discussion, resentments resurface and soon the four men are arguing as usual over property. Proctor and Corey are aligned against the grasping Putnam. Proctor and Parris dislike each other. Putnam resents the Nurses because they are successful and years earlier supported a Reverend Burroughs for minister instead of Thomas Putnam's brother-in-law. The argument ends with Reverend Hale's arrival. Proctor takes his leave; he knows witchcraft is not behind Betty's fit. But the others remain to watch Hale at work. They meanwhile reveal seeming symptoms of witchcraft. They tell Hale that Ruth cannot eat, Betty tries to fly, and the girls were dancing. Ann confesses her plan to contact her dead children. Hale prepares to treat Betty, and Rebecca departs disturbed. Betty does not respond so Hale questions Abigail. Her replies prompt him to summon Tituba. Parris and Putnam threaten Tituba with whipping and hanging. Hale promises her salvation, and Abigail betrays her, telling the group the forest rites were Tituba's idea. Terrified for her life, Tituba tells the men what they want to hear and at their prompting names other witches. When Hale tells Tituba that God will bless her, Abigail cries out that she too wants to be saved. She identifies other witches, and Betty joins in adding more names. Everyone is astounded. Parris praises God and Putnam summons the marshal. Hale requests iron chains. On this ominous note, the curtain falls.

Act 1 introduces the audience to the main characters of the play and reveals that Salem—repressive, divided by bitter rivalries, and hiding secrets—is ripe for trouble. Themes of guilt, betrayal, deception, jealousy, hysteria, hypocrisy, individual conscience, and group responsibility make their appearance here. Mention of words like "heat" and "fire" suggest that the hysterical anger which has been seething under the surface of Salem is at last erupting. They also hint that the characters are about to endure their own personal crucibles or trials by fire. It is not clear who will survive the coming storm.

Act 2: Private Lives

Just over a week later, the Proctors are preparing dinner. Their farm is on the edge of town, and though the setting seems cozily domestic there is an air of tension. The couple discuss the news from town. Deputy Governor Danforth has come to lead the trials, and more have been accused. Elizabeth wants John to warn the court that Abigail is a liar. John is reluctant and Elizabeth suspects it is because he still cares for Abigail, hence the tension beneath their conversation.

Mary Warren returns having neglected her work to attend the trials. She gives Elizabeth the poppet she stitched in court and describes how thirty-nine women were arrested. Sarah Good confessed and sent her spirit to torment the girls. Goody Osborne is to hang for refusing to confess. Proctor is disgusted. He forbids Mary to return to court but she defies him. He is about to whip her when she reveals more shocking news. Elizabeth was suspected of witchcraft but thanks to Mary no accusation was made.

After Mary goes to bed, Elizabeth and John discuss Abigail, convinced she mentioned Elizabeth in court. Elizabeth knows Abigail wants her dead and insists John makes a final break from the girl instead of giving her false encouragement. As they argue,

Reverend Hale arrives with news that Rebecca Nurse is under suspicion. He asks why John avoids church and his youngest child is unbaptized, and makes him repeat the Ten Commandments to prove his piety. Proctor recites all but the one he broke—that forbidding adultery. At Elizabeth's urging Proctor explains how Abigail admitted the outcry has nothing to do with witchcraft. Hale fears the Proctors doubt witches exist, a serious sin against church doctrine. He points to the arrests and confessions as proof of the existence of witches. Proctor suggests that when the alternative is hanging, people are bound to confess. Giles Corey and Francis Nurse burst in: Their wives have been arrested. Within a few minutes, Ezekiel Cheever and Marshal Herrick arrest Elizabeth, using as evidence a needle that apparently stabbed Abigail. They find a needle stuck in the poppet Mary made.

Proctor tries but fails to prevent the arrest. He is furious that accusers are assumed to be innocent. Hale urges him to think of any secret sin that might be the root of the troubles and leaves, followed by Giles and Francis. Proctor, guilt-ridden, resolves to reveal his adulterous affair and insists Mary Warren tell the court she, not Elizabeth, made the poppet and stuck the needle in it. The curtain falls on a sobbing Mary who declares she cannot.

The madness just surfacing in act 1 has spilled out over the town. At home the Proctors avoid it but the outside world intrudes anyway destroying their peace. From now on, they become public property. Part of Proctor's struggle will be to stand by his beliefs in the face of group pressure. Characters and themes introduced in act 1 develop further. The Proctors' relationship is revealed in images of cold, and John's guilt will drive his later actions. Rebecca's arrest hints that Salem is doomed. As Proctor points out, "vengeance is walking Salem."[24] Hale's declaration that "[If] Rebecca . . . be tainted, then nothing's left to stop the whole green world from burning"[25] is intended to calm his emerging doubts and the others' fears but will instead prove prophetic.

Additional Scene for Act 2: A Secret Meeting

Proctor summons Abigail to meet in the forest after dark. He has heard rumors that Abigail meets Danforth at the tavern and is followed around by boys. Abigail says she is serving God now. She shows him the needle marks where, she says, Elizabeth pricked her.

Proctor sees she must be insane to be taking her own lies seriously.

Abigail plans for their future together. Proctor cuts her short. He warns her to withdraw her accusations or he will ruin her. Abigail thinks his wife made him say that. She cannot believe Proctor will reveal their adultery. She tells him she will save him from himself, and departs leaving him deeply disturbed.

This scene is usually omitted from the play. Most directors feel Abigail already has motive enough for her actions. The scene suggests Abigail loves Proctor but also hints at madness. Madness removes her responsibility for her future actions, making her a somewhat weaker character

In this photo from a 1964 stage production, John Proctor comforts Elizabeth.

as a result. Again images of heat and fire are used, this time to describe the emotions that Proctor introduced into Abigail's life.

Act 3: Where Is Justice?

At the Salem Meeting House the General Court is sitting. Martha Corey is on trial. Giles tells the court that Thomas Putnam is behind the accusations. He reveals that Putnam is buying up land taken from the accused. Francis Nurse tries to convince Deputy Governor Danforth that he is mistaken in suspecting Rebecca. Then Proctor and Mary arrive. Proctor tells Danforth Mary is willing to testify that the girls lied. Danforth is cautious. The state maintains that the girls are God's mouthpiece. Contrary testimony would threaten the court's credibility and therefore the government's authority and his own reputation. Even though Proctor is not on trial, Danforth questions him about his religious practices and reveals that Elizabeth is pregnant and so cannot be hanged until after the child is born. He asks whether Proctor persists in pressing his charge. When Proctor does, Danforth's manner becomes chilly and businesslike.

Proctor, however, still believes the court is seeking truth and justice. He produces a document signed by ninety-one people supporting the good name of Elizabeth, Rebecca, and Martha. Parris and Hathorne are alarmed by this threat to their authority. Danforth orders the ninety-one people arrested for questioning.

Giles again tells Danforth about Putnam, but will not name the witness who heard Putnam boasting about his success. He does not want this witness arrested too. Danforth declares the court in session and Giles in contempt. Giles now understands where Danforth's loyalties lie and warns Proctor. Danforth himself has explained what is at stake: "Do you know, Mr. Proctor, that the entire contention of the state in these trials is that the voice of Heaven is speaking through the children?"[26] and "[a] person is either with this court or he must be counted against it, there be no road between." [27] But Proctor will not listen; he is desperate to save Elizabeth, believing it is his fault she is in jail.

The Salem witch trials began when young girls accused townswomen of witchcraft. Here, a hysterical accuser speaks with Deputy Governor Danforth.

Ever since Rebecca's arrest, Hale has had doubts about the legal proceedings. He wants Proctor to hire a lawyer. Danforth argues that with an invisible crime only the witness's testimony matters, so a lawyer would be useless. Danforth hears Mary's testimony and summons the other girls. Danforth does not believe Abigail capable of attempting murder. When Proctor reveals that the girls danced in the forest, Danforth is dismayed.

Hathorne asks Mary to deliberately faint, just as she did with the girls. She cannot, which casts doubt on her new testimony. Abigail takes this opportunity to intimidate Mary. She and the girls pretend Mary is sending spirits against them. Mary panics. Fearing for Elizabeth's life, Proctor seizes Abigail and confesses their adultery, revealing Abigail's wish to see Elizabeth dead. Danforth summons Elizabeth because Proctor says she never lies. He asks Elizabeth if Proctor has been unfaithful and Elizabeth tells a lie in order to protect John. Danforth dismisses Elizabeth and calls Proctor a liar. Hale protests and is about to denounce Abigail when she and the other girls again pretend to see Mary's spirits. They mimic Mary and she becomes hysterical too. She describes how Proctor hounded her to sign the devil's book and swore to overthrow the court.

Danforth is horrified and Proctor is so furious he can hardly speak. He warns Danforth that they will all end in hell because they all know the truth. "For them that quail to bring men out of ignorance, as I have quailed, and as you quail now when you know in all your black hearts that this be fraud—God damns our kind especially, and we will burn, we will burn together!"[28] Danforth orders him arrested along with Giles and Hale resigns from the court.

Act 3 shows public officials privately motivated to maintain personal power and reputation. The legal system as a source of justice collapses. Hoping to restore justice and atone, Proctor shatters his own reputation by publicly confessing private sins. When Mary Warren comes to testify, the tension mounts. The audience desperately wants her to stop the horror. When she breaks down, the audience, Proctor, and Hale give up this last hope that Salem can be saved. The accusers have gone too far now to turn back. There is a sense of unavoidable doom.

Act 4: Last Chance for John Proctor

Fall has arrived. In prison, Tituba and Sarah Good have apparently lost touch with reality and seem to believe the devil is coming to take them

In this scene from the National Theatre of London production, the Proctors are reunited in prison.

to Barbados. In Salem property has fallen into disrepair, crops rot unharvested, and cattle and orphans roam the streets. After months of trials, unrest is spreading to other towns and Danforth is nervous. He cannot afford to have people question his actions. Abigail and Mercy have run away with Parris's savings. If news of this gets out, there could be an uprising because executions were carried out on the testimony of thieves and liars.

Hale has lost faith in the legal system. He begs the accused to confess falsely to save their lives. When they refuse, he begs Danforth to stop the executions. Danforth will not, despite the evidence that Abigail lied. Hesitation will show church doubt, suggest the executed were innocent, and destroy the court. Confessions, however, would convince people the church acted rightly. He agrees Hale should ask Elizabeth to change her husband's mind. Elizabeth does not want to influence Proctor's actions but agrees to see him.

Husband and wife are reunited. John has heard no news in prison. Elizabeth tells him that at least one hundred people have confessed and Giles Corey is dead, pressed to death because he would not plead either guilty or not guilty. Under the law, this guaranteed his property could not be auctioned and his sons would inherit. Being apart has shown the couple how much they love each other. When Elizabeth tells John that she too is to blame for the troubles in their marriage, John decides to confess so that he and Elizabeth can have a future together. The judges are delighted. Rebecca is brought in. Danforth hopes the others will confess once Proctor does. Instead, Rebecca is shocked. She cannot confess to a lie.

Proctor is ashamed but still prepared to confess. But he refuses to accuse anyone else. The others who confessed also accused others, hoping to prove their loyalty to the church. Danforth compromises; Proctor need only sign his confession. Proctor signs reluctantly but refuses to hand the document over. The church can display a signed confession as proof they were right and the deaths justified. But it is also evidence that he, Proctor, supports the church's actions and the deaths. When he realizes this he destroys his confession. There are some things he cannot stoop to. He cannot save his life by suggesting innocent people deserved to die. He understands at last that even if he is more sinful than people like Rebecca, he is not totally evil, only flawed and human. He did not deserve his earlier reputation as a moral man, but he does now. He has finally managed to live according to his ideals. Armed with new self-knowledge, he no longer seeks to preserve his reputation out of fear of public condemnation, but rather out of respect for the integrity of others. Hale urges Elizabeth to change her husband's mind, but she refuses and the accused are hung.

By the end of act 4, the madness has run its course. Justice has failed and innocence has been lost. The trials, which could have been avoided through common sense, honesty, and decency, have brought out the worst in many people. Even where it brought out the best, as it finally did in John Proctor, it is a sad victory, for innocent people have suffered. The damage done cannot be repaired or undone, only learned from. The community built with such hopes has been shattered and left to stand as a warning.

CHAPTER FOUR

The Cast of Characters

The characters in *The Crucible* balance personal wishes against other people's expectations. They fall into one of three general groups, based on their actions: Some do what is right in spite of pressure from those around them; some give in to their neighbors' wishes; some claim they are acting for the public good but their motives are actually selfish. John Proctor is the exception; he is a member of all three groups at different points in his search for self-knowledge.

For convenience, the characters are listed alphabetically.

Ezekiel Cheever
A minor character, Cheever lives in Salem. He is a tailor by trade, and honest according to Giles Corey. He takes his appointment as clerk of the court seriously. He believes witches are truly at large in Salem. Awed by the powerful men conducting the trials, he dutifully arrests the accused.

Giles Corey
Eighty-three-year-old Giles, stubborn, rebellious, blunt, and energetic, plays an important supporting role in the play. He has had little need for books as a Salem farmer. His wife Martha's taste for reading puzzles him so much that it even distracts him from his newly learned prayers. His ill-judged frankness on the matter to Reverend Hale gets Martha arrested for witchcraft. He cannot save her, and will not accuse others to save himself. But he thwarts his neighbor Thomas Putnam's greedy ambitions for Corey's land. After frequent court appearances, Giles knows the court cannot seize his land if he refuses to enter a plea. He refuses even under

the torture of heavy stones placed on his chest. His dying words are "More weight."[29] Corey's comical traits endear him to the audience. His pain over betraying his wife earns audience sympathy. The combination of human weakness and strength makes his death moving. Critics Claudia Durst Johnson and Vernon E. Johnson suggest "the brief story of Corey may be called . . . a parallel plot to Proctor's echoing . . . his own death."[30]

Deputy Governor Danforth

Danforth is deputy governor of Massachusetts and plays a major role in the events that unfold in Salem. In his sixties, he is described as grave and sophisticated, with a hint of a sense of humor. He oversees the witch trials and believes himself to be fair and just. There is no doubt in his mind that he is doing right, making him perhaps the most frightening character in the play. He appears cultured, reasonable, trustworthy. Reverend Hale is sure Danforth will see justice is done.

Proctor too assumes that Danforth seeks justice. But beneath Danforth's suave exterior hides a man so afraid of losing power that he betrays his duty toward truth and justice. He is convinced the devil and witches exist yet uses this belief as an excuse to hang people he suspects are innocent. It is important to him always to be seen as strong and right. With honesty and humility he could perhaps have been a great man, for he demonstrates some admirable qualities. But pride transforms his intelligence into certainty that he is always right. Dishonesty prevents him from examining his motives. His determination becomes rigidity, and unlike Reverend Hale or John Proctor, he lacks the courage to admit his mistakes. Like Abigail Williams, his ideal is survival at any cost. But while her passionate nature makes her dangerous, it is his indifference to others which makes him deadly. He demonstrates what happens when an individual is granted unlimited power over those around him by those around him. Here too he resembles Abigail Williams, although her power is more limited than his.

Sarah Good

A minor character, Sarah is a penniless social outcast in Salem, making her an easy target. She is one of the first accused of witchcraft, and confesses to save her life.

The townspeople presume Danforth (right) to be a just man. In actuality, his pride and fear of losing power outweigh his sense of duty to the villagers.

Reverend John Hale

A major character, Hale, in his late thirties, is a minister dedicated to hunting out witches. Summoned by Reverend Parris to discover what afflicts Parris's daughter, Hale arrives armed with books and eager to put the devil to flight. Rebecca Nurse and John Proctor warn him that what Salem needs is someone who can restore good sense. But he dismisses their advice, too proud of his scientific learning to respect anyone else's point of view. He realizes too late that it is vengeance, not the devil, loose in Salem. Shocked and dismayed that his actions have caused destruction rather than healing, he tries but fails to save the lives of the accused. He journeys from complete faith in himself to utter despair.

He comes to Salem determined to save the town, but with little interest in the actual people who live there. As he gets to know them, and as he discovers the injustice of the legal system, his emotions take over. Now it is not a town but real people he wants to save, but his compassion comes too late. He is bewildered by a world that is not ordered and rational after all. People suffer unjustly, good is not always rewarded, emotion is not tidy, evil sometimes triumphs. He thought he understood the irrational world, but this hidden side of life sweeps him away. His personal integrity is swamped by the immoral and insane actions of those around him. His old principles become meaningless, leaving him adrift and unable to trust in any ideal at all, and so he cannot understand why Proctor and Rebecca are prepared to die for their beliefs.

Although Hale has the courage and integrity to admit his mistakes, he draws only horror and despair from the truth. This contrasts with the play's hero Proctor who accepts his true self and finds peace. But then Proctor does not have to live with the knowledge that his naïve yearning to remake the world into a paradise was in fact unconscious arrogance and destroyed the very town he thought to save. Hale takes on a crushing burden of guilt similar to the one Proctor once carried. It is not at all certain he will bear the weight. Although he is not the hero of the play, his transformation makes for fascinating drama.

Judge Hathorne

Hathorne, in his sixties and a Salem native, is described as bitter and remorseless. A supporting character, he presides over the trials and wholeheartedly supports Deputy Governor Danforth. He wants to preserve the court's power and his own position and willingly signs the death warrants of the condemned.

Marshal Herrick

Herrick, in his early thirties, is marshal of Salem. Assisted by Ezekiel Cheever, a clerk of the court and fellow Salem native, he arrests his neighbors. Both he and Cheever protest that they are bound by law to do their duty. They illustrate how injustice is carried out with the cooperation of many, not through the unaided actions of one individual. Herrick and Cheever probably see themselves as decent men who face an unpleasant task. In reality they are accomplices in a horrifying act of injustice. They are minor characters, ordinary everyman types; through them Miller suggests that evil is not something only evil people do. Everyone is responsible when evil is done, whether it is through indifference, reluctance to speak out, or active participation, because the end result—injustice and suffering—is the same. By the final act, Herrick appears to realize his complicity; he takes to drink. Cheever, on the other hand, remains a businesslike aide to Danforth and Hathorne. However, it is Herrick who escorts Proctor to his death.

Hopkins

Hopkins, a guard at the jail, is a minor character who makes only a brief appearance in the play. He is an example of someone who supports injustice by doing his job without questioning whether it is right or wrong.

Mercy Lewis

A supporting character, Mercy is maid to Thomas and Ann Putnam. She is described as fat, sly, and—ironically, given her name—merciless. She takes part in the forest rites discovered by Reverend Parris. Like the other girls caught dancing, she makes accusations to avoid punishment. She also threatens those who endanger her. She hits Ruth Putnam to waken her out of her trance, and intimidates Mary Warren to stop her exposing the girls. This use of violence mirrors the court's use of torture to influence Giles Corey, John Proctor's threats to Mary Warren, and the state's attempts to force innocent people to confess or die. In the end, she and Abigail flee the town with money stolen from Abigail's uncle, Reverend Parris.

Francis Nurse

Francis is Rebecca's elderly husband. A supporting character, he is a successful and highly respected landowner. This, and the fact that his children have survived while those of their neighbors the Putnams have not, arouses envy in the Putnams. Some years before, the Nurses also championed a Reverend Burroughs for minister of Salem instead of Thomas Putnam's brother-in-law. When Rebecca is accused of witchcraft, Francis bravely challenges the court, even though Danforth tells him he has sent four hundred people to jail and condemned seventy-two to hang.

Rebecca Nurse

Rebecca, seventy-two, white haired, and making her first entrance leaning on a walking stick, makes only a couple of appearances in the play, but they establish her as a woman of good sense and courage. She is one of the play's more important supporting characters. Wife of wealthy Francis, she is known even beyond Salem for her good works and wisdom. The Putnams envy the Nurses for their land and their healthy children. Their hatred finally destroys Rebecca when they accuse her of witchcraft. It is Rebecca who speaks out against the madness infecting Salem, warning Reverend

Parris that bringing in Reverend Hale will set everyone arguing. That such a person could hang for witchcraft reveals the insane hysteria gripping Salem and the difference between law and justice. John Proctor admires her pure motives, but she is so completely good that he feels he must be completely bad. Finally he sees he is not a demon to her saint; just an ordinary human being.

Unable to stop the madness, Rebecca meets her fate with dignity. She refuses to betray others to save herself.

Betty Parris

Betty is Reverend Parris's ten-year-old daughter, who lives with her father and her cousin Abigail Williams. Her mother is dead and her father seems more concerned with his own professional standing than the welfare of his daughter and his ward. When Reverend Parris discovers Betty, Abigail, Mercy Lewis, Ruth Putnam, and other girls from the town dancing in the forest, Betty and Ruth take to their beds, apparently unconscious. Betty's father prays by her bedside and summons Reverend Hale to examine her, fearing the devil is loose in Salem, and it is this scene which opens the play and paves the way for the hysteria to follow. Like the other girls, Betty accuses others of witchcraft both from hysteria and to avoid punishment. She is a supporting character whose fainting spell at the beginning launches the action of the play.

Reverend Samuel Parris

Parris is minister of Salem and an important supporting character in *The Crucible*. Now in his mid-forties, he was formerly a businessman in Barbados and still spends his time thinking about money. His materialism is one reason why certain of his parishioners, including John Proctor, dislike him. Parris tries to guarantee his job security by demanding the deed to the minister's house, and delivers fierce sermons about damnation in an effort to intimidate his congregation into respecting him. Even though Massachusetts is a theocracy governed by God, Parris is angry that he is not revered as God's representative in Salem. Already paranoid, he is horrified to think the devil has come to Salem through his daughter. He fears the villagers will deem him an unworthy minister and force him to leave.

To protect himself he is prepared to take advantage of others. He uses violent threats to control those in his power and flatters those with power over him. He summons Reverend Hale against

Rebecca Nurse's advice; she warns him that only trouble and division can result. He wholeheartedly supports Deputy Governor Danforth, Judge Hathorne, and the court, hoping to protect his position. When Abigail robs him and runs away he fears the parish will turn on him. It shows some courage on his part to go against Danforth and urge him to delay the executions, but it is the courage of desperation; someone left a dagger for him to find, hinting that he can expect violence if he does not do something to stop Rebecca and Proctor being hung. Parris abandons any course of action that endangers him. To his credit, he took in his orphaned niece Abigail, and it cannot be easy raising a daughter alone. But he made a poor job of teaching them morals; he taught them to protect themselves at any cost.

Elizabeth Proctor

Elizabeth is John Proctor's wife and a major character in the play. The couple live with their two young sons on a farm on the outskirts of Salem. Elizabeth considers herself plain and unlovable.

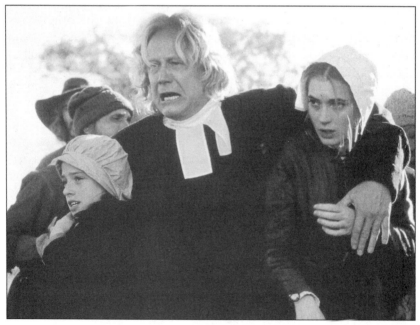

In this movie still, Reverend Parris embraces Abigail and his daughter (left). Parris is one of several characters who abandons his integrity during the witch trials.

She has also earned a reputation for honesty. Elizabeth's coldness is constantly mentioned, but mostly by John Proctor and Abigail Williams who make somewhat unreliable witnesses. Only seven months previously, Elizabeth discovered that her husband seduced their maid Abigail. John blames Abigail for tempting him with her beauty and her sinful passion, and Elizabeth for being a cold wife. But Elizabeth's coldness seems to consist of low self-confidence combined with a sincere attempt to be a good Puritan wife and mother in a society that offers her no other alternative. Her actions show her to be courageous and loyal, and she gives John the space to make his own choices. This suggests an unconditional and genuine love on her part. The fact that she loves John suggests there must be something in him worth loving. Usually honest, she lies to protect her husband only to accidentally betray him.

John Proctor

Hero of the play, John is a successful farmer in his mid-thirties, with a wife, young children, and a reputation for honesty. It helps him conceal the fact that he seduced his seventeen-year-old maid. Critic Neil Carson points out, "He is so convincing in pleading his 'honesty' that we tend to overlook the fact that he is continually lying to his wife."[31]

Proctor struggles with guilt, partly because he betrayed his wife, but mainly because his actions do not match his image of himself. Had he not seduced Abigail, events might have taken a different course in Salem. Failing that, had he confessed his adultery to Salem from the start and exposed Abigail's jealous motives, perhaps he could have prevented the hysterical witch-hunt. But he cannot bear to lose his good name and his neighbors' respect. His pride makes it difficult for him to accept being ordinary and flawed. If he cannot be as pure as Rebecca Nurse then he assumes he must be evil and "not worth the dust on the feet of them that hang."[32]

Proctor has an idealized image of himself, almost a role: that of honest farmer. It is hard for him to match this with the reality: He is also a man who lusted after a child and betrayed his wife. The contrast throws him off balance. He is forced to create a new set of values that allows room for both his emotional and idealistic sides. When he stops deceiving himself he achieves the stature he longs for. He becomes great by becoming ordinary, by accepting that he is

John Proctor (left) is pictured here with Deputy Governor Danforth and Mary Warren at the height of the witch frenzy. Proctor redeems himself by accepting responsibility for his actions.

human. Finally able to make choices driven by his integrity, instead of to preserve a public image, he chooses not to sell his soul to Salem.

Ann Putnam

Ann, aged forty-five, a supporting character in the play, is married to Thomas Putnam, a grasping landowner who harbors ill will toward many of his neighbors. She is described as a twisted person who thinks constantly of death. Of the eight children Ann and Thomas have had, only Ruth has survived infancy. Ann blames witchcraft for the deaths and is worried that she may lose Ruth who is becoming increasingly withdrawn. She sends Ruth into the forest with Tituba and the girls of Salem to ask the spirits of her dead children who their murderer is. Ann's inability to bring healthy lives into the world tortures her just as Hale's failure to bring healthy spiritual life to Salem tortures him. The Putnams envy the Nurses who have healthy children, material success, and public respect.

Ruth Putnam

Ruth, a minor character, is the only surviving child of Ann and Thomas Putnam. Her seven brothers and sisters died in infancy, and her mother has a morbid fear that Ruth may die too. Her father is obsessed by petty resentments and property disputes with his neighbors. After Reverend Parris discovers the girls of Salem dancing in the forest at night, Ruth, along with Betty Parris, falls into a strange fit that sets off the hysterical witch-hunt. Ruth is described by her mother as becoming increasingly withdrawn prior to the fit. She is little more than a pawn manipulated by her parents so that they may achieve their own ends. She goes to the forest at her mother's urging and testifies at the trials with the other girls so that her father can buy up the land of the accused.

Thomas Putnam

Thomas, an important supporting character, is nearing fifty and married to Ann Putnam. He is a greedy, vindictive, corrupt landowner involved in long-running bitter property disputes with his neighbors, especially Giles Corey, John Proctor, and Francis Nurse. He also holds a grudge against Francis because years before Francis opposed the hiring of Thomas's brother-in-law for the post of minister of Salem in favor of another candidate.

Of Thomas's and Ann's eight children, only their daughter Ruth has survived infancy. When she is caught dancing in the forest at night with the girls of Salem and falls into a fit, it sets off a hysterical witch-hunt. Thomas takes unscrupulous advantage of the witch trials to buy up the land of the accused at auction, encouraging his daughter to accuse people whose property he covets. The thorn in his side is the Nurse family. He feuds with them and envies their social, domestic, and material success, seeing in that success a constant reminder of his own failures. Giles Corey manages to thwart Thomas's bid for Corey land by refusing to enter a plea when he is accused by the court. Because Giles dies before pleading guilty or not guilty, his land cannot be auctioned and goes instead to his sons. Thomas shows no remorse for his active role in encouraging and profiting from the witch-hunt tragedy.

Tituba

Tituba is Reverend Parris's Caribbean slave. Brought to Salem against her will, homesick, isolated, and abused, she is now in her forties. The audience is given a glimpse of the vicious brutality trapping her in Salem. When Abigail falsely accuses Tituba of proposing the witchcraft ceremony in the forest, the assembled group automatically believes Abigail. Parris threatens to whip Tituba to death if she does not confess. Thomas Putnam insists she should be hanged at once. Parris is taken aback to discover her strong, negative opinion of him: "Oh, how many times [the devil] bid me kill you, Mr. Parris! . . . He say . . . Mr. Parris no goodly man, Mr. Parris mean man . . . he bid me rise out of my bed and cut your throat!"[33]

Tituba has no protection in Salem and must depend on quick wits to survive. When Hale, Parris, and Putnam question her she denies their accusations at first. But when Abigail shifts the blame to her, Tituba quickly looks for hints from the men to learn what she must say to save her life. Although her life is harsh, Tituba has spirit; and like Abigail she is a survivor. However, in the end, imprisoned for months in inhuman conditions with fellow accused Sarah Good, Tituba apparently takes refuge in fantasy, waiting for the devil to come and take her home to Barbados.

Susanna Walcott

Susanna works for Doctor Griggs of Salem. She arrives at Betty Parris's bedside with a message from her employer: He cannot find any medical explanation for Betty's fit. A minor character, Susanna is described as nervous, hurried, and slightly younger than Abigail

Tituba dances in the forest. Fortunately the Caribbean slave has a resilient spirit, for she has no one to speak on her behalf during the witch trials.

Williams. She joined in the forest dancing that preceded Betty's fit. Later she names witches. The girls of Salem can be viewed as scheming and immoral for accusing others to save themselves, but they did not go into the forest to start a witch-hunt. More likely, they wanted to escape briefly from the stifling restrictions of their daily lives through a secret, defiant act. It is the threat of death which drives them to invent the witch story, and they are not the only ones to make accusations or profit from them.

Mary Warren

Seventeen-year-old Mary is described as lonely, naïve, and subservient. A supporting character, she works for the Proctors and was one of the girls present during the forest rituals, although she insists she did not actively participate. She is not a strong personality, being readily influenced by people more dominant than she is. But as the witch trials catapult the girls of Salem from menial to exalted status, Mary is emboldened, requesting that John Proctor treat her with more respect. She even defies her employers by attending the trials when she should be working. But she is loyal too. When Abigail hints that Elizabeth Proctor is a witch, Mary is quick to defend Elizabeth, in effect saving her life.

At one point, the fate of all of Salem seems to rest in her hands after John Proctor succeeds in persuading her to confess before the court that the girls lied when they made their witchcraft accusations. Of all the girls, Mary seems the one most vulnerable to hysteria. A life rejected by her peers seems to her a fate worse than an afterlife in hell. That she should come so close to ending the witch-hunts only to falter at the last moment makes the audience realize how much they have been longing for a hopeful outcome.

In many ways, Mary's struggle mirrors John Proctor's. They both fear public censure, and they both have an understanding of what right behavior is. Each opts for what they value most: Proctor choosing integrity over compromise, Mary favoring relationship over isolation.

Abigail Williams

Abigail is the seventeen-year-old niece of Reverend Parris and former servant to the Proctors. A major character, she is traditionally considered the villain to John Proctor's hero. Beautiful but deceptive, she is commonly viewed as callous, lustful, and evil, motivated only by

Abigail Williams's desire for revenge sets in motion much of the action of The Crucible.

jealous revenge. However, her behavior suggests that she is rather more complex: a deeply scarred person with an overwhelming need to protect herself from further harm. Her parents were murdered before her eyes when she was a child. She has had to make her home with a repressive uncle who holds over her head the debt that she owes him. She is seduced by an employer twice her age and is fired for it. She cannot get another job because her seducer's wife has indicated in church that Abigail is a sinner.

John Proctor is the first person to pay attention to Abigail, and, as critic Susan C.W. Abbotson points out, her actions suggest that she is "sincerely in love"[34] with him. When he rejects and abandons her, Abigail does not want to accept it. She blames Elizabeth as the obstacle between herself and John. Her desire for revenge unleashes the hatreds and fears seething beneath the surface in Salem though she is not the cause of those hatreds. Abigail is strong-willed, rebellious, manipulative, and determined. She has a survivor's talent for seizing opportunities, but is willing to sacrifice other people in order to protect herself—a great flaw, for many innocent people suffer for it.

The final note that Abigail stole money, ran away to Boston, and was last heard of doing business as a prostitute is usually viewed as proof of her heartless immorality. But the fact remains that in seventeenth-century Puritan New England, a woman without education, family, or recommendations from a previous employer would not be offered work and would have little choice but to resort to prostitution, exposing herself to violence and deadly disease in order to feed and shelter herself.

CHAPTER FIVE

Literary Analysis

A rthur Miller wrote *The Crucible* in the mid-twentieth century, and three and a half centuries separate us from the Salem it describes. Yet it remains relevant because it does more than simply tell a story from history or talk about politics in the 1950s. It explores what it means to be part of a community, an experience shared by people from all cultures and eras. As Miller critic John H. Ferres states, "If *The Crucible* is a social play, . . . it applies to all societies rather than to any particular one. . . . [Although] Miller is careful to show how personal interest can infect society, the play seems less concerned now with a social condition than with a moral dilemma that continues to be part of the human condition for each one of us."[35]

The characters face serious choices between doing what they know to be right and doing what other people expect or want them to do. For some, doing right means risking death, and doing what others expect means having to live with the guilt of acting against one's conscience. This choice is very painful for them, and not everyone is able to live up to their best self. The audience, moved and horrified, watches until the final curtain and emerges understanding the delicate balance between civilization and chaos—and how personal choices are always shifting that balance first one way, then the other.

The Individual and the Group

Perhaps the most difficult choice a person can make is between doing what is right and doing what others want. John H. Ferres suggests that "Miller believes a man must be true to himself and to his fellows, even though being untrue may be the only way to stay alive."[36] In Salem, some charged with witchcraft avoid death by falsely accusing others. Others refuse to implicate anyone else, even if they must hang for it. Those who defend the innocent find themselves accused too.

Salem plunges into chaos because the self-serving choices of some individuals open the way for the church-led government to step in. John Proctor's adultery, Abigail Williams's bid for revenge, Thomas Putnam's greedy attempts to secure more land, Elizabeth Proctor's lie to the court to protect her husband, Deputy Governor Danforth's chilling refusal to halt the executions despite new evidence, all these private choices play their part in the destruction of Salem. It is impossible to separate the individual from the group.

The play's setting illustrates this lack of privacy. Stage directions specify that rooms are dimly lit by small windows. This creates a mood of claustrophobia, of feeling trapped. The curtain rises on Reverend Parris's home. Gradually, townsfolk intrude, gathering downstairs (offstage) but ominously audible to the characters upstairs (onstage). From there, the setting shifts to the Proctor home, and again this personal space is invaded by outsiders. This time, a resident, Elizabeth Proctor, is removed against her wishes by officials representing the town. The safety and privacy of the home has proven to be an illusion. From this point forward, the characters appear only in public settings, their independence from the group denied.

However, the more the group tries to control the individual, the more the individual feels he has to make his own choices about how to behave. So although the physical setting shifts from private to public areas, the emotional focus

In The Crucible, *Miller emphasizes his belief that one must always act with integrity.*

of the play shifts from the general hysteria of the town to one person, John Proctor, and his personal struggle with conscience.

Miller himself was to face a struggle similar to John Proctor's three years after *The Crucible* was produced. His friend and coworker Elia Kazan named him as a possible Communist sympathizer, and HUAC ordered Miller to appear before them. They wanted him to name other sympathizers. Miller was willing to talk about his own beliefs, but he refused to discuss the beliefs of anyone else. He could not in all conscience betray his friends and acquaintances or go against his own beliefs about what is right and what is not. He felt that even though every person has to live as part of a group—society—each should still try to be the best individual he or she can be.

The Price of Betrayal

Alongside this idea of the individual tied to the group, which is shown in the play and in Miller's life, is the related theme of faith and the breaking of it. All the damaging choices made in the play involve betrayal at some level. In the name of righteousness, neighbors falsely accuse each other of witchcraft. Reverend Hale, entrusted with protecting the town from evil, allows his religious zeal to blind him to what is really wrong in Salem: that people are weak, greedy, frightened, and too strictly controlled. Reverend Parris, likewise entrusted with Salem's spiritual health, betrays that trust when he places money and reputation above religion. Deputy Governor Danforth, charged with bringing justice, instead delivers its opposite and hangs innocent people in order to protect his reputation. He even encourages people to betray each other, just as two and a half centuries later, Senator Joseph McCarthy would ask people to name people whom they suspected of being Communists.

John Proctor betrays his wife Elizabeth when he commits adultery with Abigail, and again when he blames Elizabeth for driving him to it. He betrays Abigail first by seducing her, then by rejecting her, and then by blaming her for his betrayal of his wife. Even Elizabeth's lie to the court is a betrayal, both of John and of herself. She has never lied until that moment, but that one moment of breaking faith, intended to protect her husband, condemns him instead.

There are no small lies. Perhaps the subtlest example of this in the play is the moment when we first see John and Elizabeth together. Elizabeth knows John has committed adultery and she no longer trusts him. John wants her to forgive him for breaking faith with her, so he tries to think of things he can do or say that might please her. In their first scene onstage together, he tells her that she has seasoned their dinner of rabbit stew well. In truth, unknown to her he has added salt to the stew to improve the flavor. He is telling her what he thinks she wants to hear, not what is true. But trust is not something to be tricked out of someone. It must be earned, otherwise it is not trust but gullibility.

However, this never seems to occur to Proctor. Elizabeth even ends up agreeing with him that her behavior drove him to betray her. Miller critic Neil Carson points out:

> [*The Crucible*] puzzles some readers and spectators. . . . While it is clear from Miller's comments, as well as from the text, that the playwright intends us to be critical of Proctor, it is practically impossible not to see him as a martyr. There are many reasons for this. . . . Elizabeth . . . seems narrow and pinched in spirit . . . [and it] is hard not to see things from [Proctor's] point of view. He is so convincing in pleading his "honesty" that we tend to overlook the fact that he is continually lying to his wife. . . . Abigail is portrayed as such an obviously bad piece of goods that it takes a clear-eyed French critic [Marcel Aymé] to point out that Proctor was not only twice the age of the girl he seduced, but as her employer he was breaking double trust. Furthermore, the extent of Abigail's sexual awakening suggests that before her affair with Proctor she was a virgin.[37]

Yet, Proctor repeatedly labels her a whore, that is, a person who sells her body, usually to more than one person. Proctor seems more concerned that he has been guilty of the sin of lust than that he has abused the trust of his wife and of the girl in his care. Yet he accuses Abigail of being too passionate, and Elizabeth of not being passionate enough.

The Importance of Reputation

If Proctor does not see this as a problem, then it raises the question of *why* he wants Elizabeth's good opinion. Is it because he truly values it, or is it because he cannot bear to be seen as the imperfect person he is? This is a point upon which the whole play turns. Proctor's reputa-

John Proctor calls Abigail a whore in this movie still. Throughout the play, he is obsessed with his act of adultery and with his reputation among the townspeople.

tion matters to him. He is not so very different from Reverend Parris or Deputy Governor Danforth in this respect. But whereas they acknowledge it, Proctor struggles because he is also idealistic; reputation is important to him but needs to be backed up by decent behavior, and when he breaks faith with others he breaks faith with himself. As Elizabeth points out, "John, it come to naught that I should forgive you, if you'll not forgive yourself. It is not my soul, John, it is yours."[38]

This difference between how Proctor would like to be seen, and who he really is, is extremely painful to him. He recoils from this pain instead of thinking about its cause, and so misses an opportunity to learn more about himself. Critic John H. Ferres reminds us that "Miller believes . . . a man must strip away the disguises society requires him to wear."[39]

Proctor is shocked to realize how much he relies on the good opinion of others, for he has always prided himself on his independence. Perhaps he is also frightened, for he is relying on people who are, largely, not dependable. He unwillingly admits how much other people's opinions matter to him in the play's climactic scene, when Danforth asks him why he will not sign his name to his confession: "PROCTOR, *with a cry of his whole soul:* Because it is my name! Because I cannot have another in my life! Because I lie and sign myself to lies! Because I am not worth the dust on the feet of them that hang! How may I live without my name?"[40]

All the lies John Proctor has told himself through the years have been stripped away. He is like the impure or base metal alchemists used to heat up in order to burn away the impurities, leaving pure gold. They would put the base metal in a small bowl, called a crucible, and heat it up so much that the metal would become burned and blackened and dead-looking—a stage called mortification. John Proctor was burned up by the crisis that happened in Salem, and his illusions about himself were taken away one by one until he thought that all that was left was something as ugly as the burned up metal of the alchemists. But in alchemy, the burned up, blackened state was important. It was a sort of death of the impurities which would then magically leave behind only the purest substance—gold that could not burn.

At the end of the play, John Proctor at last behaves with integrity.

That is what happens to John Proctor. Everything impure is revealed and burned up. He cannot lie to himself any more. It means that any choices he makes from this point on are made from the purity that comes with honesty and self-knowledge. Miller critic Neil Carson explains that "Although it seems that [Proctor] is more jealous of his worldly reputation than of his credit with God, it is this last remnant of pride that saves him. The realization that in the end he cannot publish a lie about himself convinces him that . . . if he is not as good a man as he once thought he was, neither is he entirely evil. Like most human beings, he is a mixture."[41]

Like Miller years later, Proctor chooses to keep his good name. At that moment, who he is comes into balance with how he wants to be known. He becomes the alchemist's gold: not a pure, perfect person, but a man of integrity—true to and complete within himself. He tells Hale, "You have made your magic now, for now I do think I see some shred of goodness in John Proctor. Not enough to weave a banner with, but white enough to keep it from such dogs."[42] As Neil Carson points out, "When Elizabeth says, 'He have his goodness now,' she does not mean (as it might logically seem) that the venial John Proctor has been miraculously redeemed by the brave John Proctor. She means that he has found the true core of his nature, which had been hidden beneath self-doubt and self-loathing."[43]

A Case of Self-Delusion

Proctor is not the only character to struggle with self-deception. Hale tries to apply reason to issues of faith, even though faith is by definition an unconditional belief in something that cannot be proved logically. He arrives in Salem weighted down with the authority in his heavy books, and confidently announces: "Here is all the invisible world caught, defined, and calculated. In these books the Devil stands stripped of all his brute disguises."[44]

Sheila Huftel, author of *Arthur Miller: The Burning Glass*, explains that for Hale, devil hunting is "a precise science."[45] But, as critic Stephen Fender points out, Hale's list of demons and spirits might appear as accurate as an "encyclopaedia, but at second sight we are not convinced. . . . (Why, for example, should witches be arranged according to how they travel?) . . . The audience . . . must abandon hope at this point [that Hale can save Salem]."[46] He cannot see reality clearly enough to do so.

When reason and faith are forced together, both become twisted and mixed up. The townsfolk believe a witch can send out her spirit unseen to all but her victim. So it seems to make sense that since invisible crimes can only be witnessed by the victim, the victim's words ought to be enough to condemn an accused criminal, making "the accuser always holy"[47] as Proctor bitterly points out. However, common sense—which balances reason with feeling—would also understand and remember that revenge or fear can make people lie and bear false witness. In the 1950s accusers were "always holy" too. Just to be accused of communism was enough to ruin a person's reputation. Those who named names were considered good Americans; everyone else was "un-American," which made people doubt that they could receive justice in court if they disagreed with what HUAC was doing.

Hale's blindness leads him into a crisis in which his faith in the church and the law is damaged too. He warns Elizabeth, "Let you not mistake your duty as I mistook my own. I came into this village like a bridegroom to his beloved, bearing gifts of high religion . . . and what I touched with my bright confidence, it died."[48]

All that he built his identity on has collapsed, and Hale must come to terms with the fact that he has done the opposite of what he intended; he has helped ruin Salem. The divine justice he believed he was born to hand out turns out to be murder. His agonized cry when he admits his guilt expresses his heartfelt horror: "There is blood on my head! Can you not see the blood on my head!!"[49]

Creating Reality

Hale's ability to deceive himself is a flaw in his personality. It causes him to accidentally mislead others. But some characters in *The Crucible* deliberately lie out of revenge, or greed, or fear, or the desire for power.

Thomas Putnam's main motivation is greed; he wants to buy up the properties of convicted witches. Reverend Parris is motivated by paranoia; he sees the trials as an opportunity to remove his opponents from the town. Abigail Williams also profits by lying; she avoids hanging, and she is revenged on Elizabeth Proctor whom she sees as standing between John Proctor and herself. Elizabeth Proctor lies out of fear for her husband, thinking to save him, she assures the court that he has been faithful to her. She does not learn until it is too late that he has already confessed to adultery in order to show that Abigail cannot be trusted. Elizabeth's first and only lie does a lot of damage.

Deputy Governor Danforth wants to hold on to power. It seems at first to be God's power that he wants to protect. However, when Giles Corey insists that he cannot be arrested for contempt of a hearing, Danforth's sarcastic reply, "Oh, it is a proper lawyer!"[50] suggests that the deputy governor also takes some pride in his own powerful position and guards it jealously. He is determined to continue with the hangings even though he knows there is a chance the accused may be innocent. When Hale begs Danforth to wait, Danforth's reply is frightening: "Them that will not confess will hang. . . . [The] village expects to see them die this morning. . . . Reprieve or pardon must cast doubt upon the guilt of them that died till now. . . . Know this— I should hang ten thousand that dared to rise against the law."[51] Though Danforth does not precisely lie—at least, not in the direct way that, for instance, the girls do—he carefully creates his own version of reality, setting down the rules by which he expects others to live and die. He tells the court, "Witchcraft is . . . an invisible crime. . . . We cannot hope the witch will accuse herself . . . therefore, we must rely upon her victims. . . . What is left for a lawyer to bring out?"[52]

It is the very reasonableness of his tone that makes this false logic so terrifying. There is no defense, the audience senses, against one so certain of the facts, one so convinced of his own rationality and impartiality, one so utterly powerful. The reasonable tone disguises his unreasonable, unbalanced outlook. This lack of balance is repeated when Danforth insists that there is a clear division of the people into either good or evil: "[A] person is either with this court or he must be counted against it. . . . This is . . . a precise time—we live no longer in the dusky afternoon when evil mixed itself with good and befuddled the world."[53]

This harmless-sounding version of reality causes a lot of pain because people become convinced that they must either be completely good or completely bad. And since no one can really be completely good, then they may tell themselves and others all sorts of lies in order to seem like good people. If they stop lying, they may believe, as John Proctor does, that they must after all be evil. It takes John Proctor a while to realize that he is not good or evil, just human.

Danforth has created his own version of reality and deceives not only others, but also himself. The two things—truth and justice— that he should be thinking about most are the two things he seems least concerned with. Critic James J. Martine describes Miller as "endlessly fascinated by . . . those moments when the law and justice are at odds."[54] And they are in Salem, just as they were when Miller wrote *The Crucible* and HUAC was destroying individuals in the name of saving the country by accusing them of a "crime"— communism—that was not actually illegal.

In Deputy Governor Danforth's distorted view of the world, people were either good or evil.

A Study of Power

The law, Danforth believes, is handed down by God, and therefore not to be questioned. This combining of religion with state law makes the Salem of 1692 a theocracy—that is, a place governed by God—rather than a democracy—a place governed by majority vote. In a theocracy, power rests with those who represent God on Earth, that is to say, the church. And Deputy Governor Danforth makes it clear that he has no intention of letting that power slip away.

Proctor feels the girls have taken power. "Now the little crazy children are jangling the keys of the kingdom, and common vengeance writes the law!"[55] he declares. But the girls have only as much power as the state permits them. The people they attack are not in the government. They are inhabitants in a town under suspicion by the government. They may temporarily have influence over the elders in the town, but it is a limited power that lasts only for as long as they do not promote anything contrary to the government's view of the world. The government has the real power, and the girls become its tools. Revenge might have been one of the causes for the problems in Salem, but corrupt officials in the court blame it on the devil, aware that a world without evil would not need their protection. Any suggestion that witches (and evil) do not exist is therefore silenced. Miller scholar Christopher Bigsby points out:

> When the villagers inscribe their names on a document attesting to the good character of Rebecca Nurse, whose life is at risk, their text becomes evidence of their challenge to the writ of the court. . . . When Giles Corey prepares a deposition, that text, too, is . . . interpreted as an attack on the court. . . . Mary Warren, tempted to tell the truth, to tell a story whose plot is at odds with that offered by the authorities, is intimidated to the point at which she confesses to having signed her name in the devil's book.[56]

Giles and Mary are asked to name other witches. If they do, their sin of telling their own story instead of the official one will be forgiven. In the 1950s people accused of communism were offered a similar choice. Some did name names, just as many did in Salem. Some, like Giles, remained silent even though it cost them their jobs and good name. HUAC and the Communist hunters understood, as the court did in Salem, that their power could last only as long as everyone agreed their version of reality was the true version. This is why Danforth is so determined to obtain John Proctor's signature on his confession. Miller scholar Christopher Bigsby continues, "When [Proctor] asks, 'Why must it be written?' the answer is that he must lend his name to the narrative, to the plot, which the judges indict. . . . [His] name will complete the prepared document. When he tears the paper . . . he rejects also the social text into which they would absorb him, even as he asserts [insists on] his right to interpret the world in terms of his own beliefs."[57]

The Power of Memory

Memory plays an important role in *The Crucible*, influencing how characters interpret the world. The Putnams act on long-held grudges. Elizabeth Proctor is frightened to let go of past hurts. John Proctor is haunted by guilt for his past actions. Abigail has been damaged by the murder of her parents. Reverend Hale puts too much faith in rules set down on paper by people in the past. And the entire community is frightened to change how things have always been done.

But memory can also serve as an anchor. Rebecca Nurse remembers her ideals and stays faithful to them. Giles Corey remembers the law and refuses to plead either guilty or not guilty so his sons can inherit from him. And of course, Miller himself went back to the past to produce his cautionary tale. His aim was to warn the audience that tragedy can happen again if people do not remember and learn from past mistakes. He recommends balance: a balanced approach to memory, and a respect for its power.

Not Limited to Its Time

Critic James J. Martine sums up the strength of *The Crucible*:

> The greatest writers do not merely write ideas; they write of people. . . . This is not to suggest that writers must be without . . . a central purpose, but that a writer, no matter what his or her . . . intention, cannot make speeches without compromising [reducing the power of] his or her work. The best works of the best writers . . . demonstrate that. All of the themes . . . [of *The Crucible*] . . . are dependent upon character. It is character that is . . . essential . . . to the creation of vibrant drama—and, to a certain extent, the secret to its enduring success.[58]

In the end, *The Crucible* will continue to be popular as long as audiences feel it has something to say about their own lives. Its major themes intertwine as neatly as they do in real life. And they are themes we still deal with decades after Miller courageously wrote about them: guilt and innocence, the struggle for integrity, the search for self-knowledge, the meaning of justice, the nature of power, the need for moderation. That being so, *The Crucible* may well endure for generations to come.

Notes

Introduction: A Play for All Times

1. Quoted in Christopher Bigsby, ed., *Arthur Miller and Company*. London: Methuen, 1990, p. 1.

Chapter 1: Biography of Arthur Miller

2. Arthur Miller, *Timebends: A Life*. New York: Grove, 1987, p. 113.

3. Miller, *Timebends*, p. 226.

4. Miller, *Timebends*, p. 224.

5. Miller, *Timebends*, p. 93.

6. Miller, *Timebends*, p. 203.

7. Neil Carson, *Arthur Miller*. New York: Grove, 1982, p. 10.

8. Carson, *Arthur Miller*, pp. 14–15.

9. Miller, *Timebends*, p. 121.

10. Quoted in Bigsby, *Arthur Miller and Company*, p. 2.

Chapter 2: Historical Background

11. Quoted in Frances Hill, *The Salem Witch Trials Reader*. New York: Da Capo, 2000, p. 253.

12. Quoted in Hill, *The Salem Witch Trials Reader*, p. 253.

13. Edmund S. Morgan, *The Puritan Dilemma: The Story of John Winthrop*, 2d ed. New York: Longman, 1999, pp. 62–63.

14. Quoted in Hill, *The Salem Witch Trials Reader*, p. 254.

15. Brian P. Levack, *The Witch-Hunt in Early Modern Europe*, 2d ed. Essex, UK: Longman, 1995, pp. 177–79.

16. Hill, *The Salem Witch Trials Reader*, pp. 231–32.

17. Carson, *Arthur Miller*, p. 16.

18. Howard Zinn, *A People's History of the United States*. New York: HarperCollins, 1999; reprint, 2001, p. 432.

19. Zinn, *A People's History of the United States*, p. 435.

20. Ellen Schrecker, *Age of McCarthyism: A Brief History with Documents*, 2d ed. Boston: Bedford/St. Martin's, 2000, p. 5.

21. Quoted in Hill, *The Salem Witch Trials Reader*, p. 253.

22. Arthur Miller, *Collected Plays*. New York: Viking, 1957, p. 41.

Chapter 3: The Plot

23. Miller, *Collected Plays*, p. 237.

24. Miller, *Collected Plays*, p. 281.

25. Miller, *Collected Plays*, p. 277.

26. Miller, *Collected Plays*, p. 289.

27. Miller, *Collected Plays*, p. 293.

28. Miller, *Collected Plays*, p. 311.

Chapter 4: The Cast of Characters

29. Miller, *Collected Plays*, p. 322.

30. Claudia Durst Johnson and Vernon E. Johnson, *Understanding* The Crucible*: A Student Casebook to Issues, Sources, and Historical Documents*. Westport, CT: Greenwood, 1998, p. 17.

31. Carson, *Arthur Miller*, p. 75.

32. Miller, *Collected Plays*, p. 328.

33. Miller, *Collected Plays*, p. 259.

34. Susan C.W. Abbotson, *Student Companion to Arthur Miller*. Westport, CT: Greenwood, 2000, p. 135.

Chapter 5: Literary Analysis

35. John H. Ferres, ed. *Twentieth Century Interpretations of* The Crucible: *A Collection of Critical Essays*. Englewood Cliffs, NJ: Prentice-Hall, 1972, pp. 12–13.

36. Ferres, *Twentieth Century Interpretations of* The Crucible, p. 8.

37. Carson, *Arthur Miller*, pp. 74–75.

38. Miller, *Collected Plays*, p. 323.

39. Ferres, *Twentieth Century Interpretations of* The Crucible, p. 8.

40. Miller, *Collected Plays*, p. 328.

41. Carson, *Arthur Miller*, p. 73.

42. Miller, *Collected Plays*, p. 328.

43. Carson, *Arthur Miller*, p. 74.

44. Miller, *Collected Plays*, p. 253.

45. Sheila Huftel, *Arthur Miller: The Burning Glass.* New York: Citadel, p. 126.

46. Quoted in Gerald Weales, ed., *Arthur Miller:* The Crucible—*Text and Criticism.* New York: Viking, 1971; reprint, 1996, p. 285.

47. Miller, *Collected Plays*, p. 281.

48. Miller, *Collected Plays*, pp. 319–20.

49. Miller, *Collected Plays*, p. 319.

50. Miller, *Collected Plays*, p. 295.

51. Miller, *Collected Plays*, p. 318.

52. Miller, *Collected Plays*, p. 297.

53. Miller, *Collected Plays*, p. 293.

54. James J. Martine, The Crucible: *Politics, Property, and Pretense.* New York: Twayne, 1993, p. 46.

55. Miller, *Collected Plays*, p. 281.

56. Christopher Bigsby, *Modern American Drama 1945–2000.* Cambridge, UK: Cambridge University Press, 2000, p. 92.

57. Bigsby, *Modern American Drama 1945–2000*, p. 92.

58. Martine, The Crucible: *Politics, Property, and Pretense*, p. 47.

For Further Exploration

1. Why did Arthur Miller title his play *The Crucible*? *See also* Claudia Durst Johnson and Vernon E. Johnson, *Understanding* The Crucible: *A Student Casebook to Issues, Sources, and Historical Documents.* Westport, CT: Greenwood, 1998, pp.1–3; Neil Carson, *Arthur Miller.* New York: Grove, 1982, p. 60; John H. Ferres, ed., *Twentieth Century Interpretations of* The Crucible: *A Collection of Critical Essays.* Englewood Cliffs, NJ: Prentice-Hall, 1972, pp. 17–18; James J. Martine, The Crucible: *Politics, Property, and Pretense.* New York: Twayne, 1993, p. 13.

2. In act 3 of *The Crucible*, Deputy Governor Danforth says, "Mr. Hale, believe me; for a man of such terrible learning you are most bewildered." Why is this dramatic irony on the part of Miller? (Dramatic irony results when the audience is aware of a meaning in a character's statements that the character himself is unaware of.) What does it tell us about Danforth, Hale, and the true state of affairs in Salem? What other instances of dramatic irony are there in the play? What do they reveal about the characters and their situation? *See also* Neil Carson, *Arthur Miller.* New York: Grove, 1982, pp.70–71.

3. Read act 2, scene 2 of *The Crucible*. This scene features a night meeting in the woods between John Proctor and Abigail Williams. Why is this scene often omitted from performances of the play? *See also* June Schlueter and James K. Flanagan, eds., *Arthur Miller.* New York: Ungar, 1987, pp. 70–72.

4. Arthur Miller presents a great deal of additional information in the printed text of *The Crucible* that the audiences of staged productions never see. Do these notes help or hinder understanding of the play? Why did Miller include them? *See also* Orm Överland, "The Action and Its Significance," in Robert A. Martin, ed., *Arthur Miller: New Perspectives.* Englewood Cliffs, NJ: Prentice-Hall, 1982, pp. 33–47.

5. Compare the original text of the play to the 1996 screenplay written by Arthur Miller. What changes did Miller make, and what effect do they have on our view of the characters and events of the play? *See also* "Arthur Miller on *The Crucible*," in Miller, *The Theater Essays of Arthur Miller*, eds. Robert A. Martin and

Steven R. Centola, pp. 365–67, and *Arthur Miller*, The Crucible: *Screenplay*. New York: Penguin, 1996.

6. Research some modern-day witch-hunts, not limited to the United States, targeting any people demonized and persecuted by authorities. What similarities and differences are there between the modern-day witch-hunts and that portrayed in *The Crucible*? *See also* Claudia Durst Johnson and Vernon E. Johnson, "Witch Hunts in the 1950s" and "1990s Witch Hunts," in *Understanding* The Crucible: *A Student Casebook to Issues, Sources, and Historical Documents*. Westport, CT: Greenwood, 1998.

7. In the *Student Companion to Arthur Miller*, Susan C.W. Abbotson uses evidence in the text to offer an alternative interpretation of *The Crucible*, in which Abigail Williams emerges as the true hero of the play. Using her example, reinterpret *The Crucible* presenting one or more of the following as hero: Reverend John Hale, Elizabeth Proctor, Deputy Governor Danforth, Rebecca Nurse, Giles Corey, or Mary Warren. *See also* Susan C.W. Abbotson, *Student Companion to Arthur Miller*. Westport, CT: Greenwood, 2000, pp. 134–36.

8. How are women portrayed in *The Crucible*? *See also* Wendy Schissel, "Re(dis)covering the Witches in Arthur Miller's *The Crucible*: A Feminist Reading," *Modern Drama* 37, no. 3, Fall 1994, pp. 461–70, and Jane Kamensky, *The Colonial Mosaic: American Women 1600–1760*. New York/Oxford, UK: Oxford University Press, 1995, pp. 97–117.

9. How would audience sympathies for the characters in *The Crucible* change if Miller had not raised the historical Abigail Williams's age, lowered John Proctor's, and invented a romantic relationship between the two characters? *See also* Margo Burns, "Arthur Miller's *The Crucible*: Fact and Fiction," at Margo Burns's website on 17th c. Colonial New England, www.ogram.org; Arthur Miller, introduction to *Collected Plays*. New York: Viking, 1957; and Arthur Miller, "Journey to *The Crucible*," in Miller, *The Theater Essays of Arthur Miller*, eds. Robert A. Martin and Steven R. Centola. New York: Viking, 1978, pp. 27–30.

10. "Witch Week" by Diana Wynne Jones is a modern-day fantasy about a witch-hunt at "a boarding school run by the government for witch-orphans and children with other problems." Compare

Jones's treatment of witch-hunts to Miller's, and identify similarities and differences. *See also* Diana Wynne Jones, "Witch Week," in *The Chronicles of Chrestomanci*, vol. 2. New York: Greenwillow, 2001, p. 280. *See also* David Levin, "Salem Witchcraft in Recent Fiction and Drama" and Stephen Fender, "Precision and Pseudo Precision in *The Crucible*," in Gerald Weales, ed., *Arthur Miller: The Crucible—Text and Criticism*. New York: Viking, 1971, Reprint, 1996, pp. 248–54 and 272–89.

11. Are there any witches in *The Crucible*? *See also* James W. Douglass, "Which Witch Is Which?" in John H. Ferres, ed., *Twentieth Century Interpretations of* The Crucible: *A Collection of Critical Essays*. Englewood Cliffs, NJ: Prentice-Hall, 1972, pp. 101–103, and Wendy Schissel, "Re(dis)covering the Witches in Arthur Miller's *The Crucible*: A Feminist Reading," *Modern Drama* 37, no. 3, Fall 1994, pp. 462–63.

12. How does Miller use language in *The Crucible* to evoke Salem of the seventeenth century? *See also* Alice Griffin, *Understanding Arthur Miller*. Columbia: University of South Carolina Press, 1966, pp. 74–75, and John H. Ferres, ed., *Twentieth Century Interpretations of* The Crucible: *A Collection of Critical Essays*. Englewood Cliffs, NJ: Prentice-Hall, 1972, p. 16.

13. How does Miller use images to help us to understand the characters and themes of *The Crucible*? *See also* Alice Griffin, *Understanding Arthur Miller*. Columbia: University of South Carolina Press, 1966, pp. 76–78.

14. Based on Arthur Miller's definition of tragedy, is *The Crucible* a tragedy? Why or why not? *See also* Arthur Miller, "Tragedy and the Common Man" and "The Nature of Tragedy," in Robert A. Martin and Steven R. Centola, eds., *The Theater Essays of Arthur Miller*. New York: Viking, 1978, pp. 3–9 and pp. 8–11.

15. How would you select set design, props, costumes, and lighting to help communicate the mood, themes, and historical setting of a production of *The Crucible*? *See also* Christopher Bigsby, ed., *Arthur Miller and Company*. London: Methuen, 1990, pp. 53–54 and pp. 94–95.

Appendix of Criticism

Reasons for the Witch-Hunts

All the human suffering was perpetuated in the name of religion—fighting the Devil in a holy cause to cleanse the community of the worst manifestations of evil in order to lessen God's wrath and ease his punishment of his "Chosen People." But as many people knew even at the time, there were other, more persuasive reasons for the hysteria. Some of the impetus for the witch trials came from very basic human psychology, so puzzling and frightening to a community that believed in the manifestation of the Devil—a kind of supermagician—in their daily lives. Many of the other compelling forces were less psychological and more crass, coming as they did from less mysterious forms of evil: plain human greed, ambition, self-preservation, and revenge.

On what one might term the psychological level, the witch-hunts seem to have arisen more from the mental disturbance of one grown woman (Ann Putnam) and several adolescent girls under emotional stress. This was a group of girls just entering what for then especially was a time of terrifying physical and emotional awakening with little useful adult direction or support and a great deal of guilt and repression. On top of this, they had few approved emotional outlets; the issue of their dancing in the forest is a vivid case in point. Metaphorically, they constituted a pressure cooker that finally exploded.

To cover up what they believed (with good cause) was behavior for which they would be punished, they began to divert blame elsewhere. Almost immediately, they attracted attention and gained respect by accusing people of witchcraft. The most important citizens in the area hung on the girls' every word. The Reverend Cotton Mather and others sought them out for advice. Moreover, the girls found that they had the power to affect the lives of those who had had authority over them. They literally had power over life and death.

Claudia Durst Johnson and Vernon E. Johnson, *Understanding* The Crucible: *A Student Casebook to Issues, Sources, and Historical Documents.* Westport, CT: Greenwood, 1998, p. 73.

The Inspiration Behind *The Crucible*

I knew of one man who had been summoned to the office of a network executive, and, on explaining that he had had no Left connections at all, despite the then current attacks upon him, was told that this was precisely the trouble; "You have nothing to give them," he was told, meaning he had no confession to make, and so he was fired from his job. . . .

It seemed to me . . . that this . . . social compliance, is the result of the sense of guilt which individuals strive to conceal by complying. Generally it was a guilt . . . resulting from their awareness that they were not as Rightist as people were supposed to be; that the tenor of public pronouncements was alien to them and that they must be somehow discoverable as enemies of the power overhead. There was a new religiosity in the air, not merely the kind expressed by the spurt in . . . church attendance, but an official piety. . . . I saw forming a kind of interior mechanism of confession and forgiveness of sins which until now had not been rightly categorized as sins. New sins were being created monthly. It was very odd how quickly these were accepted into the new orthodoxy, quite as though they had been there since the beginning of time. Above all, above all horrors, I saw accepted the notion that conscience was no longer a private matter but one of state administration. I saw men handing conscience to other men and thanking other men for the opportunity of doing so.

I wished for a way to write a play . . . that would . . . show that the sin of public terror is that it divests man of conscience, of himself. . . . In *The Crucible* . . . there was an attempt to move beyond the discovery . . . of the hero's guilt. . . . [It] was no longer enough . . . to build a play upon the revelation of guilt, and to rely upon a fate which exacts payment from the culpable man. I saw [guilt] . . . as a betrayer . . . but nevertheless a quality of mind capable of being overthrown.

Arthur Miller, *Collected Plays*. New York: Viking, 1957, pp. 40–41.

The Liberal Conscience in *The Crucible*

One question remains to be asked. If Mr. Miller was unable to write directly about what he apparently . . . feels to be going on in American life today, why did he choose the particular evasion of the Salem trials? After all, violations of civil rights have been not infrequent in our history, and the Salem trials have the disadvantage that they must be distorted in order to be fitted into the framework of civil rights in the first place. Why is it just the image of a "witch trial" or a "witch hunt" that best expresses the sense of oppression which weighs on Mr. Miller and those who feel . . . as he does?

The answer, I would suppose, is precisely that those accused of witchcraft did *not* die for a cause or an idea, that they represented nothing; they were totally innocent, accused of a crime that does not even exist, the arbitrary victims of a fantastic error. . . . [The] men and women hanged in Salem were not upholding witchcraft against the true church; they were upholding their own personal integrity against an insanely mistaken community.

This offers us a revealing glimpse of the way the Communists and their fellow travelers have come to regard themselves . . . the astonishing phenomenon of Communist innocence.

Robert Warshow, "The Liberal Conscience in *The Crucible*," *Commentary* 15, March 1953, pp. 265–71, in Gerald Weales, ed., *Arthur Miller:* The Crucible—*Text and Criticism*. New York: Viking, 1971. Reprint, 1996, pp. 222–23.

Arthur Miller and How He Went to the Devil

Also necessary to establish in the first scene is the atmosphere of seventeenth-century Salem. "I use words like 'poppet' instead of 'doll,' and grammatical syntax like 'he have' instead of 'he has.' This will remind the audience that *The Crucible* is taking place in another time, but won't make it too difficult to understand, which it might if I used all the old language, with words like 'dafter' instead of 'daughter.' Also, I have varied some of the facts. Actually, the girls were reported as dancing in the woods and practicing abominations. I have them dancing naked in the woods, which makes it easier for the audience to relate the Puritans' horror at such a thing to their own."

Mr. Miller has taken some other liberties with the historical facts, as he read them in the Salem courthouse and in a book written by Charles W. Upham in 1867. . . . For instance, from Abigail Williams, whose actual age was between eleven and fourteen, plus the evidence that she tried to have Goody Proctor killed by incantations, he manufactured an eighteen-year-old wench who had seduced Goody Proctor's husband. Likewise there is no specific evidence that Proctor confessed and then recanted his confession as occurs in the play, although other accused persons did so. Says the author, "A playwright has no debt of literalness to history. Right now I couldn't tell you which details were taken from the records verbatim and which were invented. I think you can say that this play is as historically authentic as *Richard II*, which took place closer to Shakespeare's time than *The Crucible* did to ours."

Henry Hewes, "Arthur Miller and How He Went to the Devil," *Saturday Review* 36, January 31, 1953, pp. 24–26, in Gerald Weales, ed., *Arthur Miller:* The Crucible—*Text and Criticism*. New York: Viking, 1971. Reprint, 1996, pp. 184–85.

Americans' Sympathy for John Proctor Is Misplaced

In 1690, an American farmer, a husband and father, after deflowering a sixteen-year-old servant, churlishly breaks with her on orders from his wife, who pitches his mistress out the door. The little victim applies herself to the puerile practices of witchcraft in the hope that her lover will come back to her, even if it costs his wife her life. In the first act we are present at the lovers' first brief meeting after seven months of separation. She proclaims her love; he doesn't listen to anything, solemnly affirms his regret, and warns the girl he has seduced that she will soon be the disgrace of the village. Now, for the working-out of the plot and meaning of the play, it is necessary that audience sympathy go immediately to the farmer on that occasion.

No doubt it is possible in Arthur Miller's work: the sympathy of the American spectator belongs to the seducer. The reasons for that preference, though inadmissible for a Frenchman, are still weighty ones. Rugged pioneer of an earlier era, one of those resolute New England plowmen who carry in their Puritan round heads the shining promises of the age of skyscrapers and the atom bomb, the farmer is an indisputable hero from the outset. He has only to step on a Broadway stage. It's as if he were wrapped in the Star-Spangled Banner, and the public, its heart swollen with tenderness and pride, eats him up. In the presence of this eminent forefather, the girl, who has given herself to him with so much passion, is nothing more than a little slut come to sully the glorious dawn of the U.S.A. Worse, she is the odious image of sin. Indeed, at no time in the play does the Puritan take account of his responsibility toward her. Pursued by remorse for having committed adultery, he shows no regret regarding his gravest shortcoming, that of having led astray a little soul who had been entrusted to him. It certainly isn't the Broadway playgoer who will reproach him for it. In the eyes of the American of today, a Puritan family in Massachusetts in 1690 is one of those good Biblical families in which the master of the house exercises prudent thrift in conjugal patience by . . . [seducing] the servant girls with God's permission.

In France, it must be said, the Bible is not much read. Then again, an American peasant doesn't excite extraordinary feeling in the heart of the Parisian public, and the fact that he lives in 1690 in no way gives him a halo. This Puritan petticoat-rumpler who dreams only of restoring peace in his household and his chance for paradise can't fail to look bad to us, and our sympathy quite naturally will go first to the seduced girl—an orphan, into the bargain, I forgot to say.

Marcel Aymé, "I Want to Be Hanged Like a Witch," trans. Gerald Weales, *Arts*, December 15–21, 1954, pp. 1–3, in Gerald Weales, ed., *Arthur Miller:* The Crucible—*Text and Criticism*. New York: Viking, 1971. Reprint, 1996, pp. 240–41.

Dialogue in *The Crucible*

Just as the characters are based on actual persons, yet "creations of my own, drawn . . . in conformity with their known behavior," says the author in his "Note on the Historical Accuracy," so their dialogue is Miller's own invention, yet modeled upon their spoken language, recorded in court and delivered from the pulpit as sermons. It is stark yet eloquent in its simple images and its cadences; it evokes a flavor of seventeenth-century Salem, but it is not a realistic echo; it is Miller's own, artistic version. He reports that, as he sat in Salem's courthouse, reading the town records of 1692, which were "often spelled phonetically . . . [by] the court clerks or the ministers who kept the record as the trials proceeded," he then, "after a few hours of mouthing the words . . . felt a bit encouraged that I might be able to handle it, and in more time I came to love its feel, like hard burnished wood. Without planning to, I even elaborated a few of the grammatical forms myself. [Arthur Miller, *Timebends: A Life*. New York: Grove, 1987, p. 336.]

In the language Miller develops from the speech patterns found in the records, the double negative is characteristic. Rebecca Nurse, accused by both Putnams of the deaths of their infants, declares in the court record: "I am innocent and clear. . . . I never afflicted no child. . . . I am as clear [innocent] as the child unborn." ["Records of Salem Witchcraft," in Gerald Weales, ed., *Arthur Miller:* The Crucible—*Text and Criticism*. New York: Viking, 1971. Reprint, 1996, pp. 368–69.]

Miller also alters the verb conjugations and tenses to conform with those of the period. Intransitive verbs become transitive—Abby threatens a reckoning that "will shudder you"—or are transformed to adjectives, as when Mary Warren complains in act 2, on her return from the court, "My insides are all shuddery." Common verbs, such as *to be* and to have, assume a seventeenth-century flavor: *be* is used for *are* and *am*, as in "be you foolish?" "I thought it were an auction," complains Proctor to Parris, describing his sermon urging ownership of his house, "you spoke so long on deeds and mortgages." With many verbs present tense indicates the past; *let you* designates the imperative.

Archaic diction is used sparingly, to create an aura of the past, by choosing simple, familiar words such as *yea* and *nay* and *goodly*. Women are addressd as "Goody" instead of "Mrs." . . . Repetition is evocative of the cadences of the Bible, as in John's first speech: "Be you foolish, Mary Warren? Be you deaf? I forbid you leave the house, did I not? Why shall I pay you?" Miller uses strong verbs to create visual imagery: "Leap not to witchcraft," Parris cautions Putnam in the first act: "They will howl me out of Salem for such corruption in my home."

Alice Griffin, *Understanding Arthur Miller*. Columbia: University of South Carolina Press, 1996, pp. 74–75.

Imagery in *The Crucible*

Nature images often relate to winter, to suggest the harshness of New England life. These lines add divine punishment to extreme suffering and exposure when pretense is stripped away. Abigail reminds John in the opening scene, "You are no wintry man." Stone is an image that recurs in the dialogue, reflecting the actual landscape as well as the hardness of Puritan life. "The devil is precise," says Hale, "the marks of his presence are as definite as stone." Miller wonders at the absence of audience appreciation of this irony. John's final words to Elizabeth are: "show honor now, show a stony heart and sink them with it!"

In contrast to the images of hardness and of cold and winter are those of heat and fire, for the central metaphor is that of the crucible, in which the heat of fire melts, transforms, and purifies. Omnipresent is the fire of Hell. John's passion for Abigail is described in terms of the "heat" of animals; he confesses to the court in act 3 that his lechery occurred "in the proper place—where my beasts are bedded." In the forest scene (in the play's appendix) Abby uses the image of fire as both purification and passion when she tells Proctor that he "burned away" her ignorance: "It were a fire, John, we lay in fire." In the first scene Ann charges that there are "fires within fires" in the town, while Parris warns that without obedience "the church will burn like Hell is burning!" When John in act 2 agrees to go to Abby, he threatens to "curse her hotter than the oldest cinder in Hell."

Some of the burning images relate to working the soil. Farmers burned large stones to make them crack, to which Proctor refers when defending himself to Elizabeth in act 2: "Were I stone I would have cracked for shame this seven month!" That green wood resists fire is alluded to in Hale's remark, "If Rebecca Nurse be tainted, then nothing's left to stop the whole green world from burning." As fire and crucible are central metaphors, the three principals—John, Hale, and Elizabeth—are tested by enduring the fire of suffering which burns away their imperfections, and they emerge as nobler purer persons.

Alice Griffin, *Understanding Arthur Miller*. Columbia: University of South Carolina Press, 1996, pp. 76–78.

Setting as Metaphor

The first two acts are set in private homes and an audience is offered parallels and differences between the two. In both houses, there is hope that the private matters within may come to an intramural resolution. On the other hand, the final two acts are set in public places, because the things that began as private affairs have burned like fires into their public venues.

Act 1 is set in a room in Parris's house in which the only access for light is a narrow window. Parris is "a widower with no interest in children, or talent with them", and the house he keeps with his slave Tituba for his niece Abigail and his 10-year-old daughter Betty reflects his personality. There is no evidence of a woman or any affection about this house. More than merely spare, it seems sterile.

In act 2, while Proctor's living room looks much like the room in Parris's house, the small differences suggest the presence of a couple, a man and a woman living there. A door opens on the fields outside. While the audience never sees them, the Proctors have three sons, the source of warm inquiry and affectionate conversation. There is in this home a sense of fecundity, of the farm and flowers, even if, for the moment, it is being thwarted.

Act 3, set in the most public of places, will bring forth the most secret, most private revelations. If the room is meant to be forbidding, there is hopeful sunlight pouring through the two high windows as the act opens. There is no such hope in act 4's Salem jail, which is set "in darkness", the darkness deepest before the final dawn on the morning of execution.

In the first act, the audience is privy to the activities within the privacy of the home of a public man, Samuel Parris, a minister. In the second act, the audience penetrates the invisible fourth wall into the privacy of a private man, Proctor; yet, as in act 1, the activity within this home turns public. The third act portrays the engagement of the private man with a powerful and forceful public man, Deputy Governor Danforth, in a public display of what had been the private man's introspective and secret dilemma. Act 4 witnesses both public display and intimate moments between man and wife in a public place and the growth of the private man into a hero.

Abigail Williams, the driving force for what happens in all four stage settings, is seen once in a private place in act 1 and once in public in act 3, then escapes all, including responsibility, judgement, association with any specific setting. The mise-en-scène, however, is only the "place" where the playwright begins.

James J. Martine, The Crucible: *Politics, Property, and Pretense*. New York: Twayne, 1993, pp. 32–33.

The Extra Scene in Act II

The extra scene was written after *The Crucible* opened on Broadway. Toward the end of the New York run (it closed July 11, 1953), before the play went on tour, Miller restaged the production and added the new scene. *Playbill* for the week beginning June 22 first lists it—as Act II, Scene 1. At that time, the present Act I was called Prologue and each of the other three acts carried a number one less than its present designation. Thus, the new scene was played as introductory to the present Act III. When the play was published in *Theatre Arts*, XXXVII (October 1953), 35–67, the scene became Act II, Scene 2, a designation used in the acting edition (New York: Dramatists Play Service, 1954). It has since been played both ways. To me, it seems obvious that it should introduce Act III, for a brief scene tacked on the end of Act II would milk away the dramatic force of Proctor's slow build to a commitment to fight the court and the rhetoric about "God's icy wind" with which he crowns his decision.

Miller wrote a second version of the insert scene for Laurence Olivier's production of the play at the Old Vic (1965), and "he [Olivier] went crazy about it." So Miller told a class at the University of Michigan. Then, despite his enthusiasm, Olivier dropped the scene. He explained to Miller: "You know really, you don't need it. It's nice when you read the play. You get an expanded view of it. But it destroyed that certain marching tempo that starts to get into that play to that place. There's a drumbeat underneath, which begins some-where—I don't know exactly where—but in a good production it starts to beat, and this scene stops the beat."

Gerald Weales, ed., *Arthur Miller:* The Crucible—*Text and Criticism.* New York: Viking, 1971. Reprint, 1996, pp. 153–54.

Redefining the Hero of *The Crucible*

[The] conventional reading of *The Crucible* is to view John Proctor as the hero, but what if we read the play in an entirely different way which makes Abigail the hero?

Consider Abigail's position: a young, orphaned girl who has been seduced by her boss (an older, family man and respected member of his society) and deflowered in an age when virginity was a prerequisite for marriage. She then gets thrown out of the house on orders from his wife, and utterly rejected. She, perhaps naïvely, tries to win back his affection, resorting to casting spells on his wife to remove her from competition. When she does meet him again, she declares her love, but is ignored and again rejected, and the man even threatens the girl whom he has ruined that he will make her a disgrace in the town. It is not until he publicly confesses their relationship that she finally attacks him, and this is to protect herself rather than a malicious act of revenge. Surely we should be sympathizing with such a character, rather than condemning her as a wanton whore.

Although many critics prefer to view John Proctor as the innocent Christian martyr who has been seduced by the devilish whore, Abigail, there is enough evidence in the play to allow for a very different reading. Why would a simple whore try to get rid of a lover's wife? Abigail, far from being irredeemably wicked, is sincerely in love with Proctor, which her actions prove. Having been awakened by her affair with Proctor from a slumbering servitude to see her potential as a human being, Abigail struggles to uncover a sense of self in a highly restrictive society. She creates for herself a position of respect, outside of the more usual marriage, by becoming the voice of accusation which all fear. She bravely refuses to accept a patriarchal society which strives to silence and denounce independent female spirits. Her gulling of the judges and eventual escape with the mercenary reverend's savings before the town turns against her depict her as victorious—a woman who refuses to be controlled and who wins herself freedom through her own quick thinking.

The concept of Puritan restriction is in clear opposition to individual freedom, and the play depicts this division with the Salem authorities being against the young girls of the town. The authorities claim themselves to be righteous (even while doing much harm), therefore, anyone going against them must be evil. But wanting freedom should not be considered evil, but natural, for any free-spirited individual. The Salem authorities represent order and security, but such come at a heavy price, and it is a price not all girls are prepared to pay. Note how often adults (including John Proctor) suggest whipping one of the young girls of whose actions they disapprove. . . .

When a society consistently restricts an individual and will not allow a person to show independence, it is effectively killing off that individual's spirit. In any land that calls itself a democracy, that person should be encouraged to attack such a society any way he or she can in order to be free of it. Therefore, given this interpretation, we should applaud rather than condemn the heroic behavior of Abigail Williams.

Susan C.W. Abbotson, *Student Companion to Arthur Miller*. Westport, CT: Greenwood, 2000, pp. 134–36.

"The Action and Its Significance: Arthur Miller's Struggle with Dramatic Form"

Miller's reluctance to let a play speak for itself became even more evident in his two attempts to add extra material to the original text of *The Crucible* after its first production in 1953. The first of these additions, a second scene in Act Two, helps to explain Abigail's behavior in Act Three, but, as Laurence Olivier told the playwright, it is not necessary. Although Abigail's psychotic character is brought out entirely in action and dialogue, in an encounter with John Proctor on the eve of the trial, and there is no suggestion of extra-dramatic exposition, the added scene is nevertheless evidence of Miller's sense of not having succeeded in making himself understood in the original version of the play.

More striking is the evidence provided by the series of non-dramatic interpolated passages in the first act, where the playwright takes on the roles of historian, novelist and literary critic, often all at once, speaking himself *ex cathedra* rather than through his characters *ex scena*. There is an obvious difference in intent as well as effect in writing an introductory essay to one's play and writing a series of comments that are incorporated in the text itself. The material used need not be different.

For example, some of the comments on Danforth in the "Introduction" to the *Collected Plays* are quite similar to those on Parris or Hale incorporated in the play. In the one instance, however, he is looking at his play from the outside, as one of its many critics, in the other he has added new material to the play and has thus changed the text.

In effect the play has a narrator, not realized as a character but present as a voice commenting on the characters and the action and making clear some of the moral implications for the reader/audience.

> Orm Överland, "The Action and Its Significance: Arthur Miller's Struggle with Dramatic Form," *Modern Drama* 18, no. 1, March 1975, pp. 6–7, in Robert A. Martin, ed., *Arthur Miller: New Perspectives*. Englewood Cliffs, NJ: Prentice-Hall, 1982.

Alternative Versions of the Witches

I am not reading another version of *The Crucible*, one which Miller did not intend, but rather looking at the assumptions inherent in his intentions, assumptions that Miller seems oblivious to and which his critics to date have questioned far too little. I, too, can read the play as a psychological and ethical contest which no one wins, and of which it can be said that both John and Elizabeth are expressions of men and women with all their failings and nobility, but I am troubled by the fact that Elizabeth is seldom granted even that much, that so much is made of Elizabeth's complicity in John's adultery, and that the victim of John's "virility", Abigail, is blamed because she is evil and/or mad. I do want to question the gender stereotypes in the play and in the criticism that has been written about it.

Let me indulge . . . for a moment in another kind of criticism, one that is a fiction. . . . Like Virginia Woolf I would like to speculate on a play written by a fictional sister of a famous playwright. Let us call Arthur Miller's wide-eyed younger sister . . . Alice Miller. In Alice's play, Elizabeth and John suffer equally in a domestic problem which is exacerbated [made worse] by the hysteria around them. John does not try to intimidate Elizabeth with his anger, and she is not described as cold or condescending. Abigail is a victim of an older man's lust and not inherently a "bad girl"; she is not beautiful or if she is the playwright does not make so much of it. Her calling out of witches would be explained . . . as the result of her fear and confusion, not her lust. There is effort made in Alice's play to create a hero at the expense of the female characters, or a heroine at the expense of a male character. John is no villain, but—as another male victim/hero character, created by a woman, describes himself—a "trite, commonplace sinner," trying to right a wrong he admits—without blaming others.

Or, here is another version, written by another, more radical f(r)ictional [fictional] sister, Mary Miller, a real hag. In it, all the witches celebrate the death of John Proctor. The idea comes from two sources: first, a question from a female student who wanted to know if part of Elizabeth's motivation in not pressing her husband to confess is her desire to pay him back for his betrayal; and second, from a response to Jean-Paul Sartre's ending for the film "Les Sorcières de Salem." In his 1957 version of John Proctor's story, Sartre identifies Elizabeth "with the God of prohibiting sex and the God of judgement," but he has her save Abigail, who tries to break John out of jail and is in danger of being hanged as a traitor too, because Elizabeth realizes "'she loved [John].'" As the film ends, "Abigail stands shocked in a new understanding."

In Mary Miller's version Elizabeth is not identified with the male God of the Word, but with the goddesses of old forced into hiding or hanged because of a renaissance of patriarchal ideology. Mary's witches come together, alleged seductress and cold wife alike, not for love of a man who does not deserve either, but to celebrate life and their victory over . . . "'men in power' . . . who create and identify with the roles of both the victimizers and the victims," men who Mary Miller would suggest "vicariously enjoyed the women's suffering."

Wendy Schissel, "Re(dis)covering the Witches in Arthur Miller's *The Crucible:* A Feminist Reading," *Modern Drama* 37, no. 3, Fall 1994, p. 470.

Chronology

1620
Plymouth Colony is founded.

1629
Calvinist merchants, lawyers, landowners form the Massachusetts Bay Company.

1630
John Winthrop is elected first governor of Massachusetts.

1639
The General Court in Massachusetts permits settlement of Salem Village.

1672–1684
Salem Village hires Reverend James Bayley, then Reverend George Burroughs, then Reverend Deodat Lawson.

1689
Reverend Samuel Parris comes to Salem.

1692
January: Betty Parris and Abigail Williams begin having fits.

February: Other girls in Salem are afflicted; they blame Tituba, Sarah Good, and Sarah Osborne.

March: The three are tried and jailed; Martha Corey, Rebecca Nurse, and Sarah Good's four-year-old daughter Dorcas are accused, tried, and jailed.

April: The accusations spread to include John and Elizabeth Proctor, Giles Corey, Bridget Bishop, and George Burroughs; twenty-six suspects are now in jail.

May: Around forty more are jailed; new Massachusetts governor Sir William Phipps arrives from England with Reverend Increase Mather bearing the colony's new charter.

June: Phipps appoints Lieutenant Governor William Stoughton as chief judge of a new court of oyer and terminer to try the accused; Bridget Bishop is tried, convicted, and hanged; Judge Nathaniel Saltonstall resigns from the court; ministers of Boston including

Increase and Cotton Mather advise caution, speed, and vigor in the trials; witch-hunt fever spreads to districts surrounding Salem; five more are accused including Rebecca Nurse who is acquitted at first, then found guilty on the urging of the judges; Phipps reprieves her, then changes his mind.

July: The five are hanged.

August: The Proctors and George Burroughs are among those tried; all are hanged but Elizabeth who is pregnant.

September: Fifteen more accused are sentenced to death, including Martha Corey; four confess and one is pregnant, and these five are spared; Giles Corey is pressed to death for refusing to enter a plea; Martha Corey and seven others are hanged.

October: The girls accuse residents of Andover and Gloucester; many confess to save their lives; the girls accuse important citizens including the governor's wife Lady Phipps; Reverend Increase Mather questions the reliability of spectral evidence; the trials begin to be publicly criticized; Governor Phipps bans further imprisonments of accused witches and dissolves the court of oyer and terminer.

1693
January: Governor Phipps reprieves three found guilty by the new superior court led by William Stoughton; Stoughton resigns.

April: In session in Boston, the General Court finds none guilty of witchcraft.

May: Governor Phipps orders release of all accused witches provided they pay their jail fees.

1697
Reverend Parris is asked to leave Salem church.

1706
The Putnams' daughter Ann apologizes to Salem Village.

1915
Arthur Asher Miller is born on October 17 in New York City to Augusta and Isidore Miller.

1917
The Bolshevik Revolution in Russia takes place in November.

1919
The American Communist Party is founded.

1929
The stock market crash and the depression hurts Isidore Miller's clothing business; the family moves to Brooklyn.

1932
Miller graduates high school; his application to the University of Michigan is turned down; he takes a job as stock clerk; begins to read literary classics.

1933
President Roosevelt introduces New Deal.

1934
Miller reapplies to University of Michigan and is accepted.

1936
Spanish civil war; Miller wins Hopwood Award at university for his first play *No Villain*.

1936–1938
Moscow Purge Trials remove Bolshevik opposition to Stalin in Soviet Communist Party.

1937
Miller wins second Hopwood Award for *Honors at Dawn* and Theatre Guild Bureau of New Plays Award for *They Too Arise*.

1938
HUAC founded; Miller graduates from university; over next five years he writes scripts for Federal Theatre Project, CBS, NBC.

1939
World War II begins; Soviet Union agrees to fight alongside Germany.

1940
Smith Act forbids teaching or advocating the violent overthrow of the U.S. government; Miller marries Mary Grace Slattery.

1941
Hitler invades the Soviet Union and the Communists join Allies; Japan bombs Pearl Harbor.

1944

Miller's journal of his army camps tour, *Situation Normal,* is published; his first Broadway play, *The Man Who Had All the Luck,* wins the Theatre Guild National Award; daughter Jane is born.

1945

The United States drops atomic bombs on Japanese cities of Hiroshima and Nagasaki; World War II ends; Miller novel *Focus* is published.

1947

The Loyalty-Security Program is created for federal employees; the Taft-Hartley Act limits labor union power and Communist leadership of unions; the Hollywood Ten hearings summon screenwriters, directors to appear before HUAC; the Hollywood Ten are fired; Miller's *All My Sons* receives New York Drama Critics Circle Award; son Robert is born.

1948

The University of Washington fires three professors; Berlin is blockaded; Communists annex Czechoslovakia.

1949

Faculty at University of California must swear loyalty oath; China becomes Communist; Soviets test atomic bomb; Miller's *Death of a Salesman* wins Pulitzer Prize.

1950

Korean War begins; Senator Joseph McCarthy claims Communists are in the State Department; McCarthyism grips nation; among those arrested for spying are Julius and Ethel Rosenberg; Miller adapts Ibsen's play *An Enemy of the People*; Miller meets Marilyn Monroe.

1951

The Rosenbergs are tried; Communists around the United States are arrested under the Smith Act.

1953

Stalin dies; the Rosenbergs are executed; Korean War ends; *The Crucible* is produced; Miller receives mixed reviews but wins Antoinette Perry Award.

1954

Senate investigates and censures Senator McCarthy; Supreme Court rules against segregated schools; State Department denies

Miller a passport, preventing him from attending the opening of *The Crucible* in Brussels.

1955
Miller's *A Memory of Two Mondays* and *A View from the Bridge* are produced; New York City Youth Board cancels Miller's contract to write a film script about young gang members, citing possible Communist ties; Miller begins relationship with Monroe.

1956
Khrushchev reveals Stalin's crimes; the Soviet Union invades Hungary; Miller testifies before HUAC, refuses to name others who attended Communist-organized meetings; Miller divorces Slattery, marries Monroe.

1957
The Soviet Union launches Sputnik satellite; Miller is tried for contempt of Congress and found guilty; Miller's *Collected Plays* is published; Senator McCarthy dies; Supreme Court limits HUAC power and overrules California Smith Act convictions.

1958
The U.S. Court of Appeals overturns Miller's contempt conviction; filming begins on *The Misfits* starring Monroe, screenplay by Miller.

1959
Miller is awarded Gold Medal for Drama by National Institute of Arts and Letters.

1961
The Misfits is released; Miller and Monroe divorce; an opera version of *The Crucible* is produced.

1962
The Cuban Missile Crisis occurs. Miller marries Ingeborg Morath; Monroe commits suicide.

1963
Daughter Rebecca is born.

1964
Miller's *After the Fall* and *Incident at Vichy* are produced.

1965–1969
Miller becomes president of PEN (International Association of Poets, Playwrights, Editors, Essayists, and Novelists); becomes

politically active internationally as well as nationally; Miller's short story collection, *I Don't Need You Anymore*, is published; *The Price* is produced; the travel journal, *In Russia*, is published.

1970
The Soviet government disapproves of *In Russia* and bans Miller's books.

1971
The Portable Arthur Miller is published.

1972
The Crucible is revived in New York; *The Creation of the World* is produced.

1975
Death of Salesman is revived in New York.

1977
Miller's travel journal, *In the Country*, is published; *The Archbishop's Ceiling* is produced in Washington, D.C.

1978
The Theatre Essays of Arthur Miller is published; Miller visits China.

1979
Miller's travel journal, *Chinese Encounters*, is published.

1980–1982
An American Clock is produced; *Collected Plays*, vol. 2, is published; *Some Kind of Love Story* and *Elegy for a Lady* are produced.

1983
Miller directs *Death of a Salesman* in Beijing, China.

1984
Salesman in Beijing is published; *Death of a Salesman* is revived in New York with Dustin Hoffman as Willy Loman; Wooster Group uses scenes from *The Crucible* without permission in their play *LSD*.

1985
Death of a Salesman is produced for television with Hoffman; *Playing for Time* is produced.

1986
The Crucible is revived in New York and Washington, D.C.

1987
Miller's autobiography, *Timebends: A Life*, is published; *Danger: Memory!* is produced.

1989
The Crucible is revived in New Haven; the Arthur Miller Centre opens at the University of East Anglia, Norwich, England.

1990
The Crucible is revived in New York and London; Miller writes screenplay, *Everybody Wins*.

1991
The Soviet Union dissolves.

1992
Homely Girl, A Life is published.

1993
The Last Yankee is produced; Miller contributes to *Censored Books: Critical Viewpoints*.

1994
Broken Glass is produced.

1995
Miller's eightieth birthday is celebrated with gala performance at Royal National Theatre, London, and gala dinner at the Arthur Miller Centre.

1996
The Crucible is released as a feature film starring Daniel Day-Lewis as John Proctor and Winona Ryder as Abigail Williams; screenplay is by Miller; Day-Lewis and Miller's daughter Rebecca later marry; Miller receives Edward Albee Last Frontier Playwright Award; revised edition of *Theater Essays* is published.

1998
Mr. Peter's Connections is produced; the revival of *A View from the Bridge* wins two Tony Awards; Miller becomes a Distinguished Inaugural Senior Fellow of Berlin's American Academy.

1999
Death of a Salesman is revived on Broadway, wins Tony for Best Revival.

2000

Eighty-fifth birthday celebrations are held at the Arthur Miller Centre in England, and at Miller's alma mater, the University of Michigan; *Echoes Down the Corridor: Collected Essays 1944–2000* is published.

2001

Untitled is produced; *Focus* is released as a motion picture; *On Politics and the Art of Acting* is published; Miller is awarded a National Endowment for the Humanities Fellowship.

2002

The Man Who Had All the Luck is revived; *The Crucible* is revived on Broadway with Liam Neeson and Laura Linney; Inge Morath dies.

Works Consulted

Major Editions of *The Crucible*

Harold Clurman, ed., *The Viking Portable Arthur Miller*. New York: Viking, 1971. Reprint, 1995.

Allan Lloyd-Smith, Tim Roderick, and Geoff Rushbrook, *The Crucible* CD-ROM. New York: Penguin, 1993. Includes interviews with Arthur Miller, the historical context of the play, text of the play, and critical analysis.

Arthur Miller, *Collected Plays*. New York: Viking, 1957.

———, *The Crucible*. Motion picture. 20th Century Fox, 1996.

———, *The Crucible*. New York: Viking, 1953.

———, *The Crucible*. 1964. Reprint, with an introduction by Christopher Bigsby, New York: Penguin, 1995.

———, The Crucible: *Screenplay*. New York: Penguin, 1996.

Robert Eugene Ward, *The Crucible*. Opera. Libretto by Bernard Stambler, based on the play by Arthur Miller. New York City Opera, October 26, 1961.

Gerald Weales, ed., *Arthur Miller*: The Crucible—*Text and Criticism*. 1971. Reprint, New York: Viking, 1996. Includes text of *The Crucible*, essays by Miller, reviews, critical analysis, and historical background.

Essays by Arthur Miller

Arthur Miller, *Echoes Down the Corridor: Collected Essays 1944–2000*. New York: Viking, 2000. Miller's essays on the theater, politics, and his life.

———*The Theater Essays of Arthur Miller*. Eds. Robert A. Martin and Steven R. Centola. New York: Viking, 1978. Miller's essays on his work, contemporary theater, and the theater's most respected dramatists.

Biographical Information

Christopher Bigsby, *The Cambridge Companion to Arthur Miller*. Cambridge, UK: Cambridge University Press, 1997. Reprint, 1999. Discusses Miller's life and work. Essays by Christopher Bigsby, Steven R. Centola, June Schlueter, and Brenda Murphy. Also includes a bibliographic essay by Susan Haedicke.

Neil Carson, *Arthur Miller*. New York: Grove, 1982. Discusses the impact of Miller's life on his work.

Alice Griffin, *Understanding Arthur Miller*. Columbia: University of South Carolina Press, 1996. Analysis of Miller's work, including *The Crucible*, and a biography of the playwright.

Sheila Huftel, *Arthur Miller: The Burning Glass*. New York: Citadel, 1965. Examination of Miller's life and his plays including *The Crucible*. Features extracts from Miller's testimony before the House Un-American Activities Committee.

Arthur Miller, *Timebends: A Life*. New York: Grove, 1987. Autobiography covering Miller's childhood, the depression years, his professional career, his marriages, experiences with HUAC and PEN, and his political activism.

June Schlueter and James K. Flanagan, eds., *Arthur Miller*. New York: Ungar, 1987. Examination of Miller's life and works, including analysis of *The Crucible*.

Literary Criticism

Susan C.W. Abbotson, *Student Companion to Arthur Miller*. Westport, CT: Greenwood, 2000. Thought-provoking analysis of Miller's work, including *The Crucible*.

Christopher Bigsby, ed., *Arthur Miller and Company*. London: Methuen, 1990. Interviews with Miller and numerous contributions by actors, directors, reviewers, and writers discussing his influence.

———, *Modern American Drama 1945–2000*. Cambridge, UK: Cambridge University Press, 2000. Study of postwar theater in America. Includes essay "Arthur Miller: The Moral Imperative."

John H. Ferres, ed., *Twentieth Century Interpretations of* The Crucible: *A Collection of Critical Essays*. Englewood Cliffs, NJ: Prentice-Hall, 1972. Essays by various critics discussing Miller's work.

James J. Martine, ed., *Critical Essays on Arthur Miller*. Boston: G.K. Hall & Co., 1979. Features a number of essays on and reviews of Miller's work, broken down by play, as well as an interview with Miller.

Wendy Schissel, "Re(dis)covering the Witches in Arthur Miller's *The Crucible*: A Feminist Reading," *Modern Drama* 37, no. 3, Fall 1994. Schissel examines Miller's portrayal of Elizabeth Proctor and Abigail Williams and concludes that the two present stereotypical images of women, and further that audience perception of John Proctor as hero requires that the women be perceived as being to blame for Proctor's unheroic actions. She offers two alternate versions of the play by fictional Miller siblings Alice and Mary Miller.

Historical Background

Paul Boyer and Stephen Nissenbaum, *Salem Possessed: The Social Origins of Witchcraft.* Cambridge, MA: Harvard University Press, 1974. Reprint, 1994. Provides a history of Salem, examines the Putnam and Parris families, discusses the clash between old and new ideals that may have contributed to the tragedy.

Laurie Winn Carlson, *A Fever in Salem: A New Interpretation of the New England Witch Trials.* Chicago: Ivan R. Dee, 1999. Suggests that an encephalitis epidemic may have been responsible for the events in Salem.

Antonia Fraser, *The Weaker Vessel.* New York: Alfred A. Knopf, 1984. Absorbing history of women in seventeenth-century England that includes section on witch trials.

David D. Hall, ed., *Witch-Hunting in Seventeenth Century New England: A Documentary History 1638–1693.* 2d ed. Boston: Northeastern University Press, 1999. Wide selection of letters, diary extracts, trial reports, and accounts of supernatural occurrences from seventeenth-century New England. Presents the background that made the hunts possible, revealing the cultural beliefs and politics of the period. Includes a chapter on Salem.

Frances Hill, *A Delusion of Satan: The Full Story of the Salem Witch Trials.* New York: Doubleday, 1995. Reprint, New York: Da Capo, 1997. Fascinating chronicle of the witch trials.

———, *The Salem Witch Trials Reader.* New York: Da Capo, 2000. Essential comprehensive resource providing trial documents, transcripts, eyewitness accounts, testimony, the changing interpretations of historians over time, and how the trials have influenced writers.

Claudia Durst Johnson and Vernon E. Johnson, *Understanding* The Crucible: *A Student Casebook to Issues, Sources, and Historical Documents.* Westport, CT: Greenwood, 1998. Provides background context for *The Crucible* using historical documents relevant to Salem and the HUAC.

Heinrich Kramer and James Sprenger, *The Malleus Maleficarum.* Trans. Montague Summers. New York: Dover, 1928. "The Witches' Hammer," a chilling witch-hunting manual written by

Dominican monks who later became notorious inquisitors. Remarkable for its hatred of women and horrifying cruelty.

Brian P. Levack, *The Witch-Hunt in Early Modern Europe*. 2d ed. Essex, UK: Longman, 1995. Detailed analysis of the roots, realities, chronology, geography, and decline of witch-hunting.

James J. Martine, The Crucible: *Politics, Property, and Pretense*. New York: Twayne, 1993. Martine discusses the literary and historical context of *The Crucible* and offers a detailed study of the play, including its structure, setting, themes, characters, and tragic aspects.

Edmund S. Morgan, *The Puritan Dilemma: The Story of John Winthrop*. 2d ed. New York: Longman, 1999. Charts the arrival of the Puritans in New England and the establishment of the Massachusetts Bay Company, explores the separatism that caused New England communities problems in the seventeenth century.

Ellen Schrecker, *The Age of McCarthyism: A Brief History with Documents*. 2d ed. Boston: Bedford/St. Martin's, 2002. Essential resource on McCarthyism; combines study of its nature and legacy with documents from the period.

Marion L. Starkey, *The Devil in Massachusetts: A Modern Enquiry into the Salem Witch Trials*. New York: Alfred A. Knopf, 1949. Reprint, New York: Anchor Books, 1989. Study of the witch trials marred by numerous substitutions of fiction for fact.

Barbara G. Walker, *The Women's Encyclopedia of Myths and Secrets*. Edison, NJ: Castle Books, 1983. Reprint, 1996. Feminist encyclopedia exploring the roots of misogyny [hatred of women]; includes section on witches, witchcraft, and the Inquisition.

Howard Zinn, *A People's History of the United States*. New York: HarperCollins, 1999. Reprinted, 2001. Comprehensive study of U.S. history from Columbus to Clinton providing information and points of view largely ignored or distorted in standard history texts.

Websites

The Arthur Miller Society: A Brief Chronology of Arthur Miller's Life and Works (www.ibiblio.org//miller).

17th c. Colonial New England with special emphasis on the Salem Witchcraft Trials of 1692 (www.ogram.org). Margo Burns's website features information on the seventeenth century and includes discussion of the historical accuracy of *The Crucible*.

Additional Works Consulted

Interviews with Arthur Miller

Steven R. Centola, ed., *Arthur Miller in Conversation*. Dallas, TX: Contemporary Research Associates, 1993. Two interviews of Miller by Steven Centola.

Richard I. Evans, *Psychology and Arthur Miller*. New York: Dutton, 1969. Discussion of the arts as a source of psychological insight into human nature, and how artists use psychology in creating their characters.

Jeffrey Meyers, *Privileged Moments: Encounters with Writers*. Madison: University of Wisconsin Press, 2000. Includes interview with Miller in which they discuss his life.

Matthew C. Roudané, ed., *Conversations with Arthur Miller*. Jackson: University Press of Mississippi, 1987. Four decades of interviews with Arthur Miller about his work. Includes his interviews with Matthew C. Roudané, John and Alice Griffin, Robert A. Martin, Richard Evans, Robert Corrigan, Richard Meyer, James J. Martine, Steven R. Centola, Leonard Moss, and Studs Terkel among others.

Literary Criticism

Christopher Bigsby, ed., *File on Miller*. London: Methuen, 1988. Compilation of reviews of the first production of *The Crucible*.

Harold Bloom, ed., *Arthur Miller*. New York: Chelsea House, 2000. Samples taken from critics' views of Miller's works, including *The Crucible*.

———, *Arthur Miller's* The Crucible. New York: Chelsea House, 1996. Samples taken from critics' views of *The Crucible*. Features a biography of Miller and analysis of the play.

Robert W. Corrigan, ed., *Arthur Miller: A Collection of Critical Essays*. Englewood Cliffs, NJ: Prentice-Hall, 1969. Essays by various critics discussing Miller's work, including Gerald Weales and Robert Warshow. Robert Corrigan's introduction discusses the achievements of Miller.

Robert A. Martin, ed., *Arthur Miller: New Perspectives*. Englewood Cliffs, NJ: Prentice-Hall, 1982. Features essays on Miller's work by Orm Överland, Thomas E. Porter, and Ruby Kohn, among others, and an introduction by Robert A. Martin.

Leonard Moss, *Arthur Miller*, 2d ed. New York: Twayne, 1980. Examines Miller's work, discusses the social and psychological aspects of his plays.

Thomas Siebold, ed., *Readings on Arthur Miller: The Crucible*. San Diego, CA: Greenhaven, 1999. Research resource featuring selections drawn from numerous critical essays on *The Crucible*.

————, *Readings on Arthur Miller*. San Diego, CA: Greenhaven, 1997. Research resource featuring selections drawn from numerous critical essays on several of Miller's plays, including *The Crucible*.

Dennis Welland, *Miller: The Playwright*, 2d ed. New York: Methuen, 1983. Study of Miller's work, including analysis of *The Crucible*.

Historical Background

John Putnam Demos, *Entertaining Satan: Witchcraft and the Culture of Early New England*. Oxford, UK: Oxford University Press, 1982. Paperback ed., 1983. Examines the social roots and impact of early New England's belief in witchcraft.

Albert Fried, *McCarthyism—The Great American Red Scare: A Documentary History*. Oxford, UK: Oxford University Press, 1997. A range of documents offering insight into the phenomenon of McCarthyism.

Jane Kamensky, *The Colonial Mosaic: American Women 1600–1760*. New York/Oxford, UK: Oxford University Press, 1995. Part of women's history series. Includes chapter featuring information about witches and Salem in the seventeenth century.

Carol F. Karlsen, *The Devil in the Shape of a Woman: Witchcraft in Colonial New England*. New York: W.W. Norton & Company, 1987. Reprint, 1998. Explores the gender bias underlying Colonial New England's witch-hunts.

J.B. Russell, *Witchcraft in the Middle Ages*. Ithaca, NY: Cornell University Press, 1972. Development of medieval witchcraft.

Ellen Schrecker, *Many Are the Crimes: McCarthyism in America*. Princeton, NJ: Princeton University Press, 1998. Account of the background and impact of McCarthyism.

Websites

Arthur Miller Forum (www.catharton.net). Online forum discussing aspects of Miller's work.

The Crucible on **Broadway** (www.thecrucibleonbroadway.com). Website dedicated to the most recent Broadway revival of *The*

Crucible, which ran for 120 performances from March 7, 2002, to June 8, 2002. Site provides background information on this and past productions, additional information on witch-hunts, and a study guide.

The Crucible **Project** (www.curriculumunits.com). Information on various aspects of *The Crucible*, including background information, clips from a production, and *Crucible*-related activities.

The Miller Society (www.ibiblio.org). Website promoting the study of Arthur Miller and his work. Organizes national conferences every one to two years; planning to launch an Arthur Miller Journal.

Salem Witch Trials Documentary Archive and Transcription Project (http://etext.lib.virginia.edu). Features court records, letters, maps, and electronic texts of archival materials.

Spartacus Educational Site—Encyclopedia of USA History: McCarthyism (www.spartacus.schoolnet.co.uk). Background information on McCarthyism and links to information on spies, informers, investigators, and those blacklisted.

Index

Picture Credits

Cover photo: © Robbie Jack CORBIS
Associated Press, AP, 12, 36, 38
© Bettmann/CORBIS, 22, 24
© CORBIS SYGMA, 72
Dictionary of American Portraits/Dover Publications, 34
© Hulton/Archive by Getty Images, 26, 31
© Hulton-Deutsch Collection/CORBIS, 21
© Robbie Jack/CORBIS, 9
Chris Jouan, 17
Library of Congress, 14, 30
Photofest, 16, 19, 40, 41, 42, 45, 46, 48, 52, 56, 58, 60, 62,
    64, 67, 68

About the Author

M.N. Jimerson received her B.A. in English from Smith College and her M.F.A. in writing from Vermont College. She has worked as a counselor with adolescent girls and adults in crisis, and has led writing workshops for children and teen parents. Her young adult fantasy *Wychwood* won the PEN New England Children's Book Caucus Discovery Evening Award. Jimerson was born in London but now lives in Massachusetts with her husband and home-schooled daughter and various energetic pets.

HOAKW   812
         .09
        M61J

JIMERSON, M. N.
   UNDERSTANDING THE
CRUCIBLE
12/04

              HOAKW   812
                       .09
                       M61J

HOUSTON PUBLIC LIBRARY
OAK FOREST